CW01583521

Wirral's Coast:

Saughall
to
Red Rocks

Walking Through History

By
Marilyn Stevenson

Front cover: 1598 County Pallatine map of Cheshire by kind permission of Wirral Council.

Every effort has been made by the author to obtain copyright permission to reproduce photographs and extracts included in this book. In the event of any omissions please contact the publisher.

First Published 2012 by Countyvise Ltd
14 Appin Road, Birkenhead, CH41 9HH

British Library Cataloguing in Publication Data.
A catalogue record for this book is available from the British Library.

ISBN 978 1 906823 59 7

Dedications

I dedicate this book to the memory of my parents Irene and Archie Prince.

This book could not have been achieved without their interest in local and family history which was so eagerly demonstrated by them during my early years.

Also a great thank you to my husband David, without his constant help, support and encouragement given over the years, the completion of this book would have only been a dream.

This includes the arduous task of walking and driving to all the locations on so many occasions, and patiently photographing our journey.

Also thanks must go to my daughters for their unstinting help and encouragement, without whose help this book would not have been completed. Karla advised me on new IT skills, updated my ancient word processor and proofread the final manuscript. Helen spent many hours walking rivers and fields, assisted with maps and research, and proofread the first draft.

Much more could be said for all my family, thank you for helping me realise my potential.

Acknowledgements

Wirral and Cheshire are fortunate to have excellent local study libraries and record offices; this book could not have been written were it not for the invaluable assistance of their staff and facilities.

I would like to thank Cheshire Archives and Local Studies (Cheshire Shared Services), Neston Library, Birkenhead Library, Wallasey Library, and Wirral Archives, Each of these bodies holds a substantial collection of documents and photographs appertaining to the history of Wirral.

Wirral Archives, located on the ground floor of the Cheshire Lines building in Birkenhead, have kindly given me permission to publish in this book, a copy of their most treasured possession; it is the 1598 map of the County Pallatine of Chester by William Smith.

To Greg Dawson a local author of five books on the history of Wirral, who has given me expert guidance on many matters regarding the writing and contents of this book.

Finally, thank you to all who gave me advice during my walks while I was conducting my research, and who have not been named.

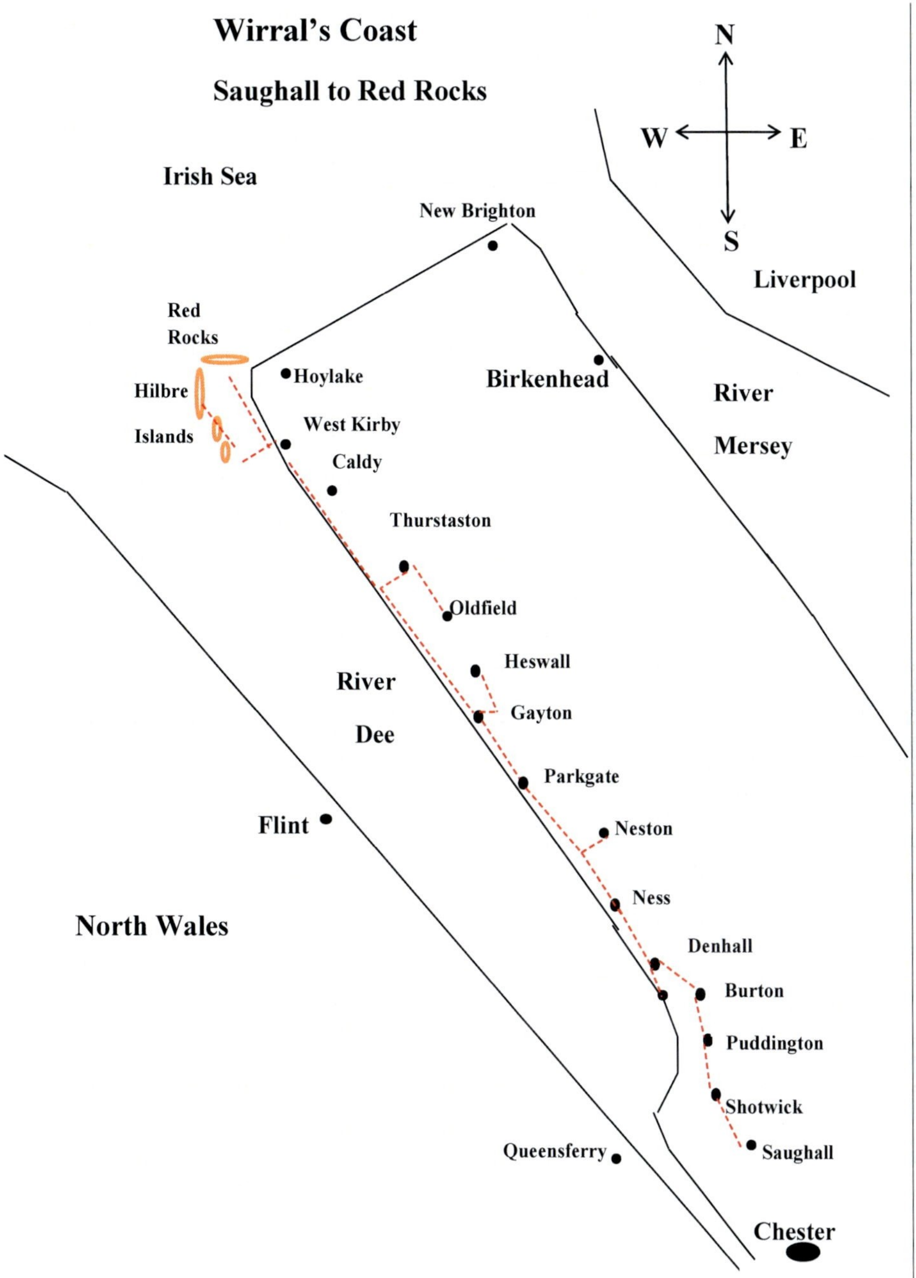

Wirral's Coast
Saughall to Red Rocks
N
W
E
S
Irish Sea
New Brighton
Liverpool
Red Rocks
Hilbre Islands
Hoylake
Birkenhead
River Mersey
West Kirby
Caldy
Thurstaston
Oldfield
Heswall
River Dee
Gayton
Parkgate
Flint
Neston
Ness
North Wales
Denhall
Burton
Puddington
Shotwick
Saughall
Queensferry
Chester

Part of the 1598 map of the County Pallatine of Cheshire. By kind Permission of Wirral Council as the owner of the copyright, no part of it may be reproduced in any material form without the written permission of Wirral Council. The original map is held in Wirral Archives.

Contents

Introduction

Wirral, ancient and modern, is a fascinating place to visit and live. It provided the perfect place for me to complete a journey, visit places new and revisit places of old.

Only now, it was a journey of a different kind, to walk from one end of the peninsula to the other, along the way gathering information which I felt would be of interest to visitors and residents alike.

A journey for me is not just visiting a place and looking at the view, but to know something of the history, geology, and of the people who once lived there. These factors were all important and gave the places I was visiting a much more interesting appeal.

The objective then was to complete the journey down Wirral's west coast and record an historical account of the places which I had visited.

This is the Wirral that I know, but you too could take your own journey and create your own memories. You may decide to complete the journey following the route shown here or visit them independently, but remember, it's the journey that matters not just the destination.

I was born in Wirral in 1949, and my memories since childhood are of quiet lanes, and meadows which we thought were there for us to play in (that is until the farmer found you). Streams were full of sticklebacks, ponds of reeds and fish, and quarries where I searched for dinosaur bones.

Old carts were stagecoaches abandoned by highway robbers, we learnt to swim in the sea dodging Portuguese men of War (jelly fish), all of this, and with an ancient submerged forest on our doorstep at Dove Point.

My first step towards researching this book was taken with my daughter Helen; it was on a cold winter's morning when we were knee deep in water, investigating the river bed of Shotwick Brook, prodding the muddy depths below our feet with a stick.

Two years have since passed, during which I have travelled from Saughall to Red Rocks, a distance covering 24 miles, along coastal paths, footpaths, lanes and byways, discovering Wirral's history and landscape along the way. The Wirral Peninsula is a geographical location and not confined by political boundaries.

This book can be read as an armchair read, or depending on time and effort can be used as a guide for walks to, and around, local points of interest.

Each chapter includes a sketch of the route though not to scale, and each walk can easily be followed with, or without, an Ordnance survey map. The following are the Ordnance Survey maps if you choose to use them:
Scale 1:50000 117 and 108
Scale 1:25000 266.

Wirral: How to get there.

Access to Wirral is served by several routes; The Queensway tunnel from Liverpool to Birkenhead, the Kingsway tunnel from Liverpool to the M53, or perhaps journey across the River Mersey by ferryboat from Liverpool's Pier Head to either Birkenhead or Seacombe.

Motorway links are via the M56 then M53, a more scenic route is from Chester on the A540, but whichever route you choose you will journey through a landscape over 208 million years old.

Wirral's Coast

Saughall to Red Rocks
Walking through History

Wirral is a Peninsula *"Paene insula"* means almost an island. Wirral is located in the North West of England, bounded by the River Dee, River Mersey and the Irish Sea. Its entire coast-line is approximately 46 miles; the peninsula's ancient southern land boundary is at the Vale of Broxton. The Shropshire Union Canal roughly follows this boundary.

'Cornovi', a Celtic tribe from central Wales and Shropshire evolved into the British Kingdom of Powys and knew the Wirral as *'Kilguri'* or the '*corner'.* They were a powerful tribe during the Bronze Age right up to the Roman period. There are a few Celtic place names found in Wirral, such as Liscard, Noctorum and Landican.

Wirral is mentioned in the Doomsday Book, written in 1086. There were 405 heads of families living here then, in 2010 the population is considerably greater.

Wirral has a long and varied history; there are only a few documents which define the southern reaches of the Peninsula, one interesting one is from John Leland who was antiquary to King Henry VIII. In 1537 he wrote,
"Wyrale begynnith lesse than a quarter of a mile of the very cite self of Chester, and withyn a 2. Bow shottes of the suburbe without the Northgate at a little brooket caullid Flokars Broke that ther is a dok wherat at spring tide a Ship may ly, and this place is caullid Porte Pool"

John Leland was born in 1503; he was chaplain and as antiquarian to Henry VIII was requested by the King to conduct a survey of England's churches and monasteries. In doing so, John Leland travelled the length and breadth of England, not just recording the churches and monasteries, but also the villages he travelled through and the roads he travelled on. (John Leland died insane in 1552).

Wirral has always been a place of great interest and worth, in 1120 Wirral's land mass was a source of great wealth for some, and abstract poverty for the masses.

Randle de Meschines IV Earl of Chester turned Wirral into a Royal Forest. 'Afforested' meant the district was a hunting ground for the nobility, and was subject to 'Forest Law'. Forest Law protected land, animals, birds, walls, fences, hedges, and trees, not the inhabitants. To the local population the 'Royal

Forest' became a serious threat to their livelihood. Heavy penalties were inflicted on them if Forest laws were broken Alan Silvester became the first Chief Forester of Wirral.

The people of Wirral petitioned Edward Prince of Wales, the 'Black Prince', with complaints of 'criminals taking refuge in the forest'. The 'foresters' themselves were breaking the law, and thus caused great harm to Wirral's inhabitants.

In 1376, the (Black Prince) began the process of disafforestation. He died 6 weeks before it was finally granted by a charter from his father King Edward III on 20th July 1376.

What else can Wirral's coast line offer the explorer? A landscape created 245 million years ago, its oldest exposed rocks are 208 million years old, therefore when you walk on Wirral's two main sandstone ridges, Shotwick to West Kirby and Bidston to Storeton you are walking on Triassic rocks. Some are coloured red with oxides of iron, some coloured yellow, they are known as Keuper and Bunter sandstones.

River Dee Bore

Wirral as a peninsula can boast of a natural phenomenon which occurs on the River Dee, and the River Mersey it is a 'Bore'

Both rivers are tidal estuaries, when high water is over 10 metres at Liverpool it can produce a running wave of water which is called a 'bore', this occurs only a few times a year.

The River Dee bore is best viewed from the old road bridge at Queensferry, about 2 hours before high water at Liverpool, then at Saltney Ferry footbridge at 1 hour and 30 minutes before high water at Liverpool, then at Chester 30 minutes later, although much reduced. In 1908 the River Dee bore was described as:
'A white capped mass of water 3 to 4ft high and moving at a rate of 7-8 miles per hour'

The River Mersey bore can also be seen in the lower estuary opposite Hale Point, about 2 hours and 25 minutes before high water at Liverpool. Liverpool and Irish Sea Tide Tables are available from local newsagents, if you are interested in witnessing this natural phenomenon.

The River Dee has seen many trials and tribulations. One amazing fact is that in 973 when Edgar was anointed king of all England, he summoned a meeting with all the Kings of Britain. To show his new found power Edgar gave a naval demonstration on the River Dee, the following kings gathered for the event: Kenneth of Alba, Donald of Strathclyde, Maccus of the Isles, Iago of Gwynedd and at least two other princes.

What a sight that must have been over 1000 years ago!

Now the journey begins, perhaps one long distance walk, or a few shorter walks as and when you can, the choice is yours.

Saughall to Shotwick Castle a walk of 3 miles

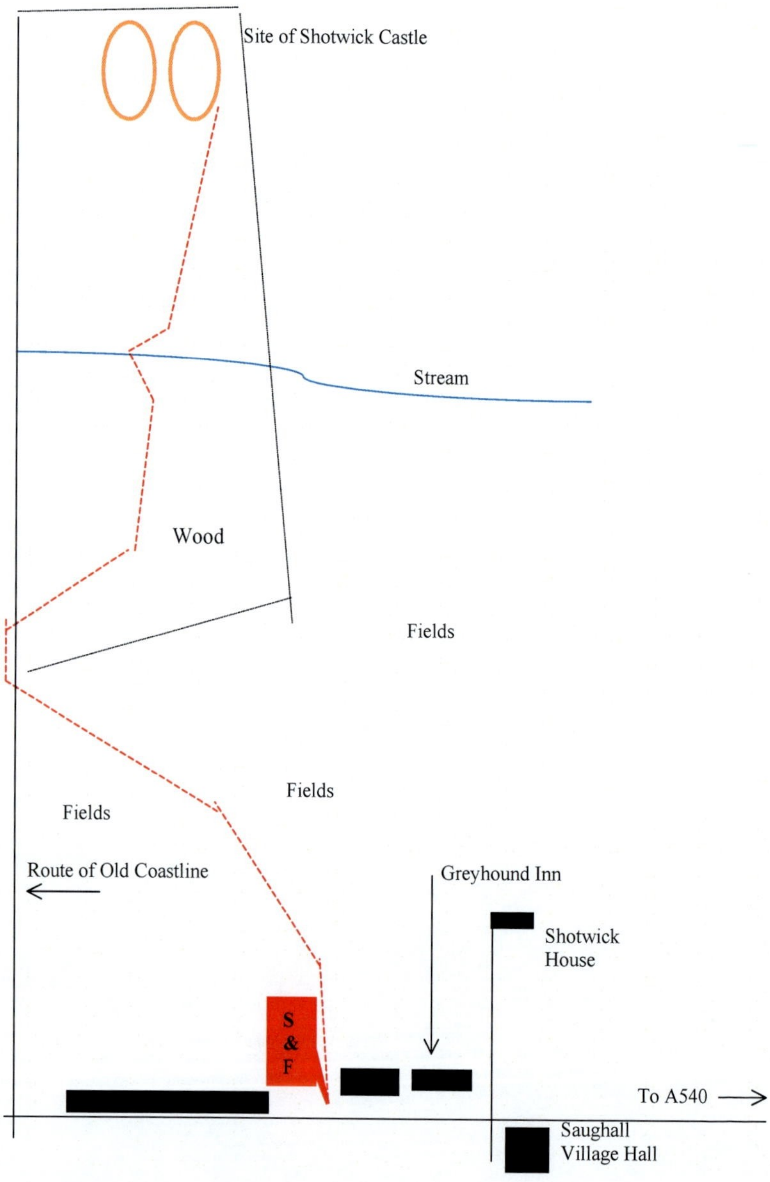

Chapter 1: Saughall to Shotwick Castle

A passage from John Leland's 'Itinerary of Wyrale' describes the location of Shotwick Castle:
'*A myle lower of Crabbo village is Shottewick Castelle on the very shore logging to the King, and thereby ys a Park'.*

A walk of 1.5 miles takes you to Wirral's only castle of antiquity, that of Shotwick Castle. Start from the village of Saughall.

From the A540, take the road directing you to 'Saughall', travel down Long Lane then cross a small junction onto Church Road.
A little further on you pass a church and a school on the right, within a hundred yards is the15th century Greyhound Inn, sadly the inn is now closed. On Seahill Road parking is available.

Just opposite the Greyhound Inn is the village hall and library. Built in 1920 it is a rather pretty building painted in a lovely shade of lilac. There are two plaques dedicated to the men who fell in action from both world wars, the plaques are located just to the left of the clock tower.

Saughall village hall and library 2011

A black and white signpost points the way to 'Welsh Road,' the sign is slightly overgrown by shrubs.

Follow the footpath up through the grassy lane and across the stile, walk a few yards and cross over a second stile, you are now on the edge of a large field, cross the field diagonally to your left, and there in the distance is another stile.

As you are crossing this field you may notice ridge and furrow marks on the ground over 3 metres in width, these are from old ploughing methods.

Once across the stile and bridge you are on the edge of another field, cross this field diagonally to your left, look out for the faint track in the grass heading off towards some trees.
There are fantastic views over the Welsh hills from here, and at the time of writing it was warm and bright with clouds scudding across the open skies.

Cross the stile, the path is short but steep and care should be taken going down. At this point you are on the 10 metre contour line. Here old Oak trees stand bent by the passage of time. Continue to the bottom of the hill, cross another stile, and turn right.

You are now on the old estuary shoreline, walk on a few yards till you come to a gate crossing the track, on your right is a wooden stile, go over the stile and climb the hill through the trees. What was once the old shore line is now open meadow and used for grazing horses.

You can hear the distant traffic on the A550 from here, once in the woods it is quiet and peaceful. It appears to be a natural wood with many old Oak trees standing high on the ridge. The path is easy to follow, carry on past the junction on the right and head straight on downhill, cross the stream then go up a set of wooden steps, keep to the path. You will soon come across a signpost pointing the way to Shotwick Castle.

Cross over the next bridge spanning a small culvert which drains the higher fields, the tree canopy opens out here, fern and brambles line the path. The tree cover returns within a few minutes, cross another bridge, the stream below has cut deep into the sandstone bedrock forming small cliffs either side of the stream.

Follow the path up, when you reach the clearing you will catch your first glimpse of the earth mounds which are the remains of Shotwick Castle.

Shotwick Castle in the 21st century

The day I visited in 2009 the earth mounds where hauntingly enigmatic, two mounds covered in grass with a trench running through in the shape of a crescent. The remains of the Castle which are evident today, are much less than were found in the 17th century.

DRAWINGS OF SHOTWICK CASTLE
(Harl. MS. 2073 (111), Randle Holme Collections)

Old drawings of Shotwick Castle. The captions read:
"the ruines of the Castle of Shotwick on the west side" (top)
"the ground plot of Shotwick Castle before it was ruinated" (bottom)

A 17th century plan of Shotwick Castle by kind permission of Cheshire Archives and Local Studies (Cheshire Shared Services) Ref C/SHOT/B

Here you have an elevated view of the Welsh hills, imagine the old shoreline, the tide lapping at the cliffs below, (10m high) a sultry haze on the River Dee, ships anchored off shore, cargoes being unloaded ready to be carted into the castle.

The building of the Norman Castle was attributed to Hugh Lupus, the first Earl of Chester, around 1080. It was part of a chain of castles to protect the area from attack by the North Welsh Princes. The castle was said to be of pentagon shape with walls of 51ft high including a 5 storey watch tower, the Motte lies on the old bank of the estuary now marked by the tree line.
The Bailey lies to the northeast; the Ditch on the western side was very wide and was suggested may have served as a dock.

The British Archaeology 'newsletter number 24', suggests that the ditch was a form of medieval garden, and that the moat was cut off from the River Dee by a late medieval dam, and that it was more of a pond than a dock. The newsletter also states that the earthworks inside the castle's bailey also appear to represent a late medieval garden.

I prefer to imagine the castle without the medieval gardens and choose the dock theory more than the pond; it's a more romantic scene.
The site was excavated in 1876 by a Mr Williams, who was a schoolmaster from Saughall; unfortunately he did not publish his findings.

King Edward I and King Henry III both visited Shotwick Castle, the last to visit in 1353 was Edward Prince of Wales (the Black Prince), son of King Edward III. The castle was probably first built of earth and timber, then in 1240-1242 it was repaired and a palisade was erected, but by1621 the castle was classed as a ruin.

All that can be seen now are grassy mounds. What must it have looked like all those years ago? Let your mind wonder as you view the terrain, it is still an impressive site even today.

I like to think that on a dark winter's day, with the mist rolling in off the fields below, you could hear the sounds of castle life as though only a few years have gone by, and not 900. The ruin would have been more impressive, but sadly in the middle of the 18th century, most of the Castle's stone was removed to make sea defences in the estuary.

Once you have wandered around the earthworks of Shotwick Castle retrace your steps back to Saughall Village.

Saughall to Shotwick a walk of 2 miles

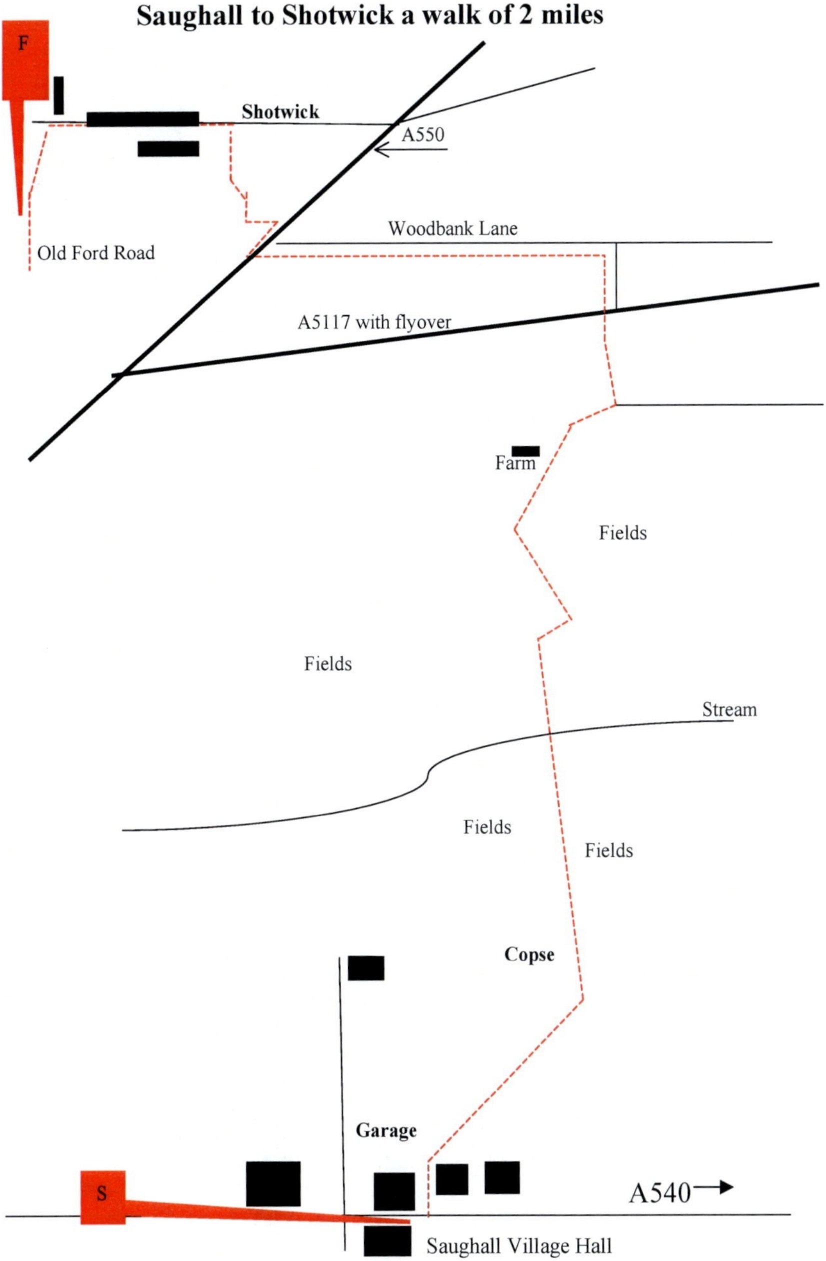

Chapter 2: Saughall to Shotwick Village

On Seahill Road in Saughall Village is the Saughall service station, on the right just after the service station is a footpath sign. The footpath is alongside a house and could be missed! Go up the footpath and through the gate, a wooden sign points the way to Shotwick '2 miles'.

Follow the track in the grass, straight across a large field, there is a small narrow copse of trees ahead, another gate leads you into the trees. Within a few metres a second gate leads you into another field, walk straight on, to your right is an old hedgerow with tall Oak trees in its midst.

Cross a farm track to a double stile, which is complete with footbridge spanning a drainage ditch, cross the wooden bridge, keep to the faint tracks in the grass, and walk uphill. At the time of writing I could hear gun fire from the rifle range at Sealand. Walk through another gate across another farm track, keep to the headland, the walk is slightly uphill, you will find the views of the Welsh hills are excellent from here.

It's approximately 20 metres above sea level here. At the time of writing a farmer was cutting grass, and within a few minutes three large trailers of grass had been cut, quicker farming methods today than the past I think.

The path drops down to the right hand corner of the field, cross over an old stone step, (from a much older stile) through the gate, cross a farm track and walk uphill. This headland path traverses a number of peaks and troughs, and is unlike the rest of the coastline on this walk.
Go through the gate which is straight ahead, not through the gate on the right, the path follows the hedgerow downhill; it crosses the stream which meanders its way towards Shotwick Castle.

Cross the stream by the double stile and footbridge, the path in summer can be difficult, long grass and nettles are your companions. Walk uphill, at the time of writing the corn is over 2 metres high, but when the crops are harvested, the now hidden view of the estuary emerges.

Cross over the next stile, then another farm track, you will see another double stile to the right. Once over the stile, turn left then follow the hedgerow, then through two gates in quick succession, once through the second gate turn right, and walk up the lane. Go through the gate which crosses the track, and walk straight on, turn right and walk towards the footbridge that spans the A5117.

Walk over the footbridge and carry straight, on ignoring the road to the right. On reaching the T junction, turn left onto Woodbank Lane; walk on until you reach the pelican lights which cross the A550.

Cross the road and turn right, walk along the grass verge; you will see a signpost pointing the way to Shotwick. Turn left onto a small path; go through the gate and across the field keeping to the right, the tower of Shotwick Church can be seen from here.

Go through another gate following in the direction of the yellow arrows, immediately opposite is another gate, go through this and walk downhill, keeping to the right of the field.

Half way down the field on the right, is a double stile, and a wooden footbridge which crosses Shotwick Brook. It is a fairly new bridge which is gated at both ends, here the brook still has its sand and stone bed, just as it does when it passes under the A550. This section of the brook is crowded with nettles, hawthorn, blackberry and brambles, the brook meanders on, searching for the River Dee.

Once across the stile the path carries on up the hill, look for the stile, it's partly hidden in the hedgerow. Cross over the stile, the path drops down to Shotwick Road, turn left, within a few minutes you will arrive in Shotwick Village.

Notes on Shotwick Village

Shotwick or "*Sotowiche*" as it was recorded in the Doomsday Book of 1086. The name Shotwick is of Saxon origin, the pretty village is situated 4 miles from Chester.

During the time that the Doomsday book was written, the church of St Werburghs held the village, and many other areas in Cheshire.
According to the Doomsday book, within Shotwick's village boundary was a hide, this was a measurement for land taxation; the name comes from Old English which was spelt *hid or hida.* A hide was generally considered to be enough land to support a household for one year.
The village paid geld on this land; geld was another Old English word for land tax.

The village had land for 3 ploughs; generally 1 plough had a team of 8 oxen. You may think that 24 oxen seem excessive, but as they were the only source of power to till the land, they were much prized. Today's farming methods include tractors, combine harvesters, tree felling equipment, ditch diggers, to name but a few. One man now usually means one machine for farmers in the 21st century. In order to till the land, you needed a workforce, Shotwick had the following:

Four *Villeins - they* were classed as high status peasants, 'customary tenants', who owned their home but were tied to the land they worked. They were not free as we know it.
Two *Bordars*- lived in Shotwick; these were a lower class of peasant than the villeins.
One of these *Bordars* held a plough; they lived on the perimeter of the village.

One advantage Shotwick held over many areas on the Wirral, was that it held one acre of meadow land, this was a valuable asset in Wirral, and was in short supply. The value of Shotwick as quoted in the Doomsday book, prior to 1066 was 16 shillings, and in 1086 it was worth only 13s.3d.

Many villages in Wirral and Cheshire where laid waste by William the Conqueror, the reason being, that Wirral and many parts of Northern England, rebelled against William's rule, and subsequently the North of England was harried by William. Hundreds of villages across England were laid waste, some did not recover, others eventually did.

Shotwick today is a tiny village tucked away off the A550 and if you travel down its tree covered lane, you enter a village lost in time.

To the left of the lane, Shotwick Brook meanders, as it cuts its way through the Bunter sandstone, and Boulder clay cliffs as it has done for over 1000 years. A tithe map records 2 fields here, named "The Cliffs".

The village grew up around a 'ford', by which travellers crossed the River Dee into Wales. In 1339 the route was called the 'Saltesway', also known as the 'Kings Highway'. Salt was carried from the salt mines of Cheshire into Wales. In 1245 King Henry III led a campaign into Wales, King Edward I campaigned in 1278, and in 1284 led further campaigns into Wales from Shotwick ford.

Just before you enter the village the tree canopy lifts, red sandstone houses stand either side of the lane, ahead is the church of St Michael [patron saint of soldiers].

I have visited Shotwick many times over the years, visiting with my mother and father when I was a young girl, it hasn't changed; perhaps there is a time warp here!

St Michael's Church Shotwick 2010

St Michael's church was built in the 12th century; it has a Norman arch in the south doorway and has had many alterations over the years.
The church is open and should be visited; you will find much more information inside the church regarding its history, much more than I could add here.

Records from Cheshire Archives and Local Studies, (Cheshire Shared Services), record the following in connection with the church:
In Chester Cathedral library, records exist of a Saxon church being built here in A.D 900, although no remains exist now.
In 1280, a survey recorded that rushes were gathered as an old Wirral custom, to place in the Lord's house or castle. Every year on May 1st churches were strewn with rushes, garlands and ribbons.

In 1616 the curate of the church was Hugh Burrows; he was recorded in the court records as;
'*Omitting prayers, not reading the service, administering communion to parishioners sitting not kneeling, and refusing to bury a corpse'*.
He was obviously having some problems at the time!

During the time of the plague at Chester, couples were married at Shotwick. Was it a healthier place to be?
Then disaster, in 1641 the plague held Shotwick in its grasp from '*Midsomer to Michelmas'*.

In 1743 the parson Mr Davis, was paid 4d for a quart of ale for taking the service.

In 1760, stones were brought from Burton at a cost of £1.1s to repair the church.

In 1763, the church interior was plastered and was painted white at a cost of £1!

There is such a varied history here, you can read many tomes, but come and sense the atmosphere; it's perfect. Don't forget to walk around the churchyard, I love it, so many tombs and headstones in disarray, as though they have been picked up and then thrown down again, as though in a game of 'jacks'.

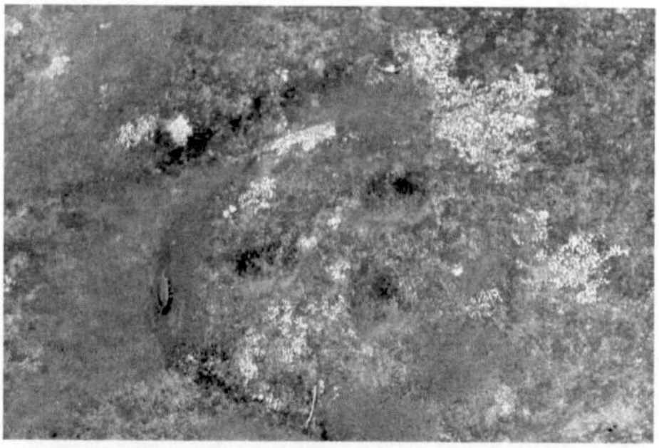

If you look carefully to the right of the main church entrance, there is a flat tombstone with the faint outline of a skull!
When I was a child the stone carving was much clearer, my imagination conjured images of the pirate Bluebeard, now it would be Captain Jack Sparrow!

At the church entrance, look at the porch's sandstone walls, to the left and right are long grooves etched into the sandstone blocks. These marks were made by archers sharpening their arrowheads; the abled bodied men of the village by law had to practise archery every Sunday after Mass.

Groove etched in the sandstone of Shotwick church porch

Armies came and boarded ships to Ireland from here when the anchorage at Chester had silted up; Shotwick Port was used for up to 100 years.

When the new cut in the River Dee was made in 1733 – 1754, it eventually led to the channels in the Dee silting up; never again will Shotwick Port witness ships in its safe anchorage, unless global warming has a surprise in store for us. Stand with your back to the church and close your eyes, imagine the River Dee a few yards away, small ships are anchored, you can hear and smell the life of a tiny port.

Now turn and face the rear boundary wall of the churchyard, to the far left of the wall you will notice, for a few feet, it is built of very large old blocks of sandstone, quite different from the rest of the Church boundary walls.

Iron ring in the boundary wall of Shotwick Church

On the top of the older wall you will notice a small iron ring partially covered by ivy, and embedded into the sandstone; the ring was believed to have been used to anchor small vessels to the wall.

A harbour was recorded being built in Shotwick between 1422 and 1471, but no trace remains of it now. On leaving the churchyard, turn right and go through the gate next to the church wall. In the woodland on your left, a culvert spouts from under the lane and heads out towards Shotwick Brook, pieces of pottery and a clay pipe have been found here under an uprooted tree .

The lane runs downhill, this is the old 'Ford' road which crossed the River Dee, notice the churchyard wall curving to the west, walk straight on downhill, at this point you are approximately 3 metres above sea level. The leafy lane now curves left and the trees recede, continue on until you reach a small stone bridge built with larger than life sandstone blocks. This is a sturdy structure for such a small bridge.

Walk straight on till you find the lane curving left again, this brings you close to the flyover and junction of the A548.
Just think of the men, women and children, who have forded the River Dee into Wales over the centuries from this very spot. Where were they going? Did they ever return? It must have been a hazardous journey at any time, dangerous mud flats, marsh, and swift flowing tidal creeks were a serious threat to life.

PART of Huddart's "The Coasting Pilot for Great Britain and Ireland, 1794."

Huddart's map of the coast at Shotwick in 1794 clearly shows the route over the marshes to Wales.

Huddart's map of 1794: by kind Permission of Cheshire Archives and Local Studies (Cheshire Shared Services) CSHOT/B

As you can see from the following archive extracts:

In 1498 William and Robert Hancock were accidentally drowned.
They came to Dee waters in a 'cokboote' laden with mussels from Caldey Skere, which they were to sell at Chester. The boat was driven inshore to Shotwick, were the boat was wrecked at 'Flodegate' a fish or floodyard.

June 26th 1707. *My wife, Mr Plumb and I came over from Holywell over Shottwigg Ford, it was very deep, thence we came to ye Woodside where we got over.*

July 10th 1721 We *came over from Holywell to Flit (Flint) thence to Shotwick where I rode over without a guide & came back again with one to fetch my wife over, then to Eastam where I left my servant and horses. My wife and I went over in the Sower-Milk Galley and landed about eleaven of ye clock at Night at Leverp (Liverpool) we lodged at the Wool-pack.*

Today in the distance you can hear the traffic on the A550 and the A548, even now this route is being expanded with a bypass and underpass, to allow more travellers to cross the River Dee into Wales, and it is a much quicker and far safer route today.

Today no tolls are due; this was not the case for many previous travellers. Port taxes were paid for goods disembarking from the ships anchored at Shotwick bound for Chester. When goods were brought through Chester's gates, tolls had to be paid!
An example of tolls taken from Chester's city gates in the year 1441 for the week beginning 6th December:

Eastgate	4d
Bridgegate	8d
Northgate	2d
Watergate	0d

Bridgegate was the gateway to Wales and was by far the busiest route into Chester.

See Appendix 1, Chester Murage Roll 1441-1442 is a detailed list of Chester's merchants and their occupations.

Retrace your steps back to the stone bridge, on the left of the bridge in the stone work is a trig point denoting an ordnance survey mark, and the initials JM. Still looking to your left you will notice the brook has been canalised, forcing the water off towards the A548, while on the right you will notice how the brook meanders past the village and towards the bridge.

The bed of Shotwick Brook consists of sand and stone before it reaches the village, but an underlying ooze of blue-black clay is found in the brook beyond the village, but prior to the bridge. This could imply the blue clay deposits found within the brook could have been tidal to that point, including the fields to the front and left of the church.
Shotwick Brook rises near the cross roads 'Burton to Willaston' on the A540, it's approximately 54 metres above sea level at that point, the brook then runs parallel with the A540 before dropping down towards Shotwick village, it's a tiny virtually unknown river system.

Return towards the village, it's had a varied history, take a look at the quaint houses, what stories can they tell:

1561 John Helwyn de Shotwick was the inn keeper of the Greyhound alehouse it was used for irregular marriages.

1663 Twenty one households were assessed for hearth tax; this was quite a prosperous village!

1674 Randel Mosse or Mosie of Prenton, and Martha his wife were unlawfully married by Mr Heath, curate of Shotwick in John Richards's alehouse (Greyhound Inn).

1677 John Robinson of Bebington and Isabella Mainwaring of Eastam, were unlawfully married by Mr Heath in the alehouse, I wonder why?

1811 Seventeen families lived in Shotwick.

1841 One hundred and twelve people lived in Shotwick, the publican of the Greyhound Inn was Hamish Booth.

Below is a copy from the Tithe map of Shotwick in 1843, together with a list of occupants and their dwellings.

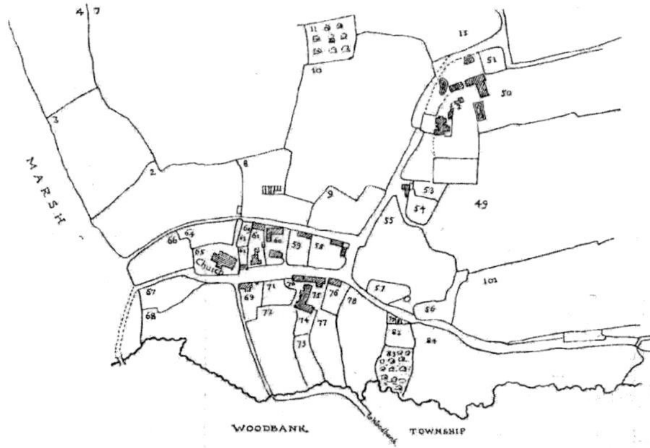

PART OF THE TOWNSHIP OF SHOTWICK
From the Tithe Map, 1843

2. SEAFIELD.
3. 4. BANKS.
7. GREAT MEADOW.
8. HOUSE AND CROFT (REV. JAMES COTTINGHAM).
9. HUGHES ORCHARD.
10. LITTLE MEADOW.
11. MOAT NURSERY.
13. RYE CROFT.
49. CINDERS.
50. COPPICE.
52. THOMAS MADDOCK, HOUSE, BUILDINGS, GARDEN.
53. WM. NEWNS, COTTAGE AND GARDEN.
54. THOMAS THOMAS, COTTAGE AND GARDEN.
55. KILN GARDEN.
56. WEBSTER'S CROFT.
58. GEORGE TRUEMAN, COTTAGE AND GARDEN.
59. REV. JAS. COTTINGHAM, BUILDINGS AND CROFT.
60. JOHN ELLIS, HOUSE, SHOP, AND GARDEN.
61. EDWARD DAVIES, COTTAGE AND GARDEN.
62. EDWARD JONES, COTTAGE AND GARDEN.
64. CHURCHYARD CROFT.
66, 67. BUTTS.
68. BROOK LOONS.
69. MARY DAVIES, COTTAGE AND GARDEN.
70. PUBLIC HOUSE [&c.].
71. GARDEN.
72. CROFT BACK OF HOUSE, SAML. ROBERTS, ALSO FARMER.
73. ORCHARD.
74. STACKYARD.
75. FICHD. DAVIES, HOUSE, BUILDINGS, GARDEN.
76. MARGT. JONES, HOUSE, BUILDINGS, GARDEN.
78. ORCHARD.
82. PINFOLD GARDEN.
83. THE BOG.
84. THE CLIFFS.
101. ARGUE LOONS.

Shotwick Tithe map 1843 by kind permission of Cheshire Archives and Local Studies (Cheshire Shared Services) C/SHOT/B

Walk up towards the houses on your right, the first house is Church Cottage. Notice the stocks in the garden, not of antiquity but nice just the same.

The second house is Greyhound Farm; this was originally the alehouse and the coroners' court. In the coroner's court, murder cases were heard. Such as:

1509 Thomas Cotyingham coroner for Wirral, noted Richard Fox of Shotwick was killed by Henry Nicholasson and Piper of *Podyington* (Puddington).
In 1513 and 1523 two more murders were heard at the coroner's court, are there ghosts afoot here!

Carry on towards Stone Cottage opposite the junction with Hall Lane, straight ahead leads you back out of the village and on to the A550.

Turn left into Hall Lane and walk past Fir Tree Cottage, which is on your left, carry straight on up the lane passing a pair of farm houses on your right.

Just a little further on you reach Shotwick Hall, built in 1662 of red sandstone, it is shaped like a letter 'E' its grand wings are either side of the main entrance; in the cellar a spring is known to rise.

Shotwick Hall 2008

Shotwick estate was the seat of the Hockenhall's, obtained by marriage at the time of King Edward I, the hall remained in the Hockenhall family until the last century; the estate was then mortgaged and sold.
It is private property, the road finishes here but the footpath to Puddington beckons. Two fields over to the left is the site of the ancient Manor house of Shotwick, now all that can be seen is a grassy mound in the middle of a clump of trees.

This ends our visit to Shotwick; the next place of interest is Puddington.
To continue to Puddington by vehicle, retrace your route to the junction of the A550 turn left, then at Two Mills traffic lights turn left onto the A540, then left again within a few hundred yards at a T junction signposted to Puddington, 1½ miles distance.

Shotwick to Puddington a walk of 1 ½ miles

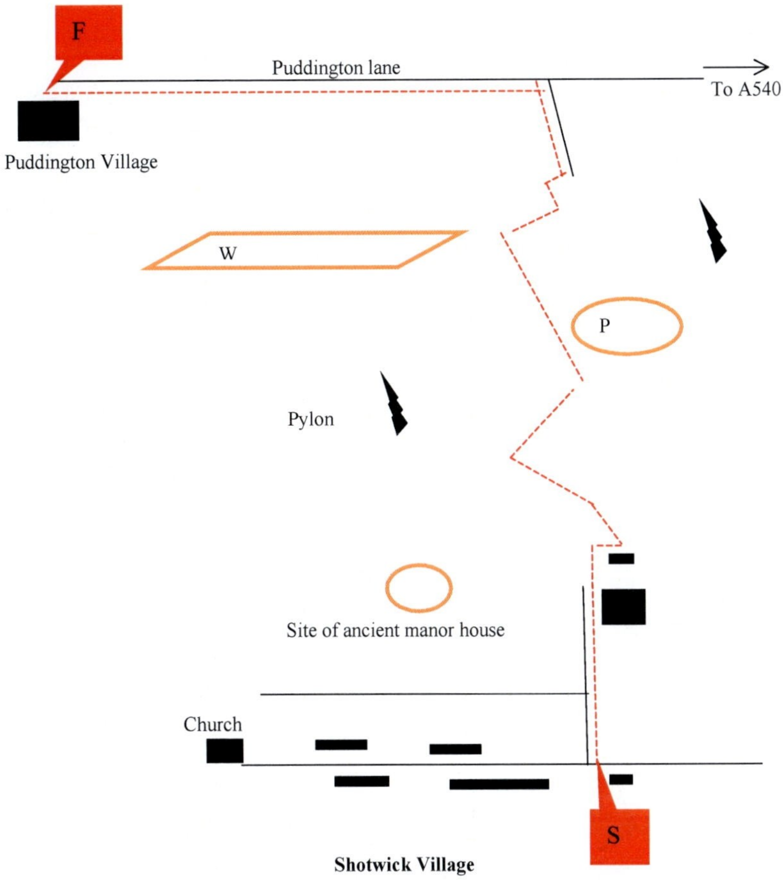

P= Pond
W=Wood

Chapter 3: Shotwick to Puddington

You can park your vehicle in Shotwick village, the walk to Puddington is approximately 1 ½ miles. Walk down Hall Lane opposite Stone Cottage, past a pair of semi-detached houses which bear a date stone of 1937.

Shortly you will pass Shotwick Hall Farm on your right; the metalled lane finishes here at the hall. Across the lane is a farm gate with a single gate on the left, go through the single gate onto a stony farm track. The track curves to the right past a barn, and then turns left along a muddy farm track.
When the muddy track appears to lead into a gated field on your right, you will notice on your left a signpost with a yellow arrow indicating the way.
Take this track as it threads its way past brambles, thorns, nettles, it's narrow but clearly visible. The original width of the track was nearly 3 metres wide, with its clay banks nearly 1 metre high, this is clearly an old footpath.

The track has been used for many years, oak, sycamore, holly, hawthorn line your way. At the end of the track is a gate, go through the gate and follow the hedge on your left to the next field boundary. Go through the opening in the hedge row, again keep left and follow the hedge row until you reach a wooden gate. Go through two gates in quick succession, turn right and walk uphill.

At the time of writing it was autumn, the field had been tilled and the heavy red clay was strewn with small stones, pebbles, quartz, slate, granite, marble, flint, shale, all shimmering in the bright sunlight. These stones are called 'erratic's', and were most probably deposited by glaciers which made their way over the Wirral from the western highlands of Scotland, and down through the Lake District. As you travel round the coast you will see other remnants of the Ice Age.

Continue uphill, glance back and look at the view, fix your eyes on the clump of trees growing in a linear line ahead and to the right. This is the old shoreline of the estuary; the trees cover the 10 metre contour line at this point. The 30 metre contour line is at the top of the hill; two pylons traverse the field and head out over the estuary to Hawarden in North Wales.

Two thirds of the way up the field you will notice a yellow sign directing you to turn left across the field.

The tithe map of 1841 records this field as the '*Great Old Park'* and the field behind you as '*Great Lodge Brow'*, perhaps this was part of the deer park belonging to Puddington Manor. Alan Sylvestre was the first Master Forester or bailiff.

Cross the field, whereupon you reach another signpost next to a large pond on your right. This is a quite secluded place; the deep pond is surrounded by bull rushes and afloat with lilies. Hawthorn, oak, and willow stand erringly on its banks, a lone fisherman tends to his net. At the far side of the pond you will notice that part of the bank falls gradually into the water, this can be typical of a Marl pit. Marl was used as a fertiliser or soil improver, its makeup was that of shale, sand, shells, *i.e. Lime.*

In 1296 the Abbot of St Werburghs was cautioned for digging Marl without permission. Marl was another remnant of the Ice Age, pockets of sand and shale were lodged in the Boulder clay and when the sand and shale were removed it left a clay bed. This then filled with water, leaving what we see today as large ponds dotted all over Wirral's fields.

Carry straight past the pond to a copse ahead of you across the field, keep to the right of the copse and the field boundary, within a few yards you will notice a farm track on your left, walk up the track then turn right opposite a farm building. Within a few yards the track joins a metalled road, turn left at this point.

The 1841 Tithe map records a Reverend Richard Gillow as occupying a property and fields here.

Follow this quiet stretch of road for a few minutes until you will reach a junction, this is the main road to Puddington. Turn left, within a few minutes you will arrive in the village.

Notes on Puddington Village

In 1086 when the Doomsday book was written, the village was recorded as '*Potitone*' A man called *Hamo held the village for Earl Hugh of Chester,* Hamo was a free man.
There was enough land for three ploughs for the villagers to farm, there were:
4 Villeins
4 Bordars
1 Slave
1 *Radman* with his own plough, *Radman* comes from Old English and means a riding servant.

The name of Puddington is an Anglo-Saxon word, and is derived from the personal name of 'Put*(t) a'* with the *ing &tun* meaning a farm or farmstead. I wonder what the man 'Put*(t) a'* was like? His name was important and has continued to this day, will ours perhaps?

William the Conqueror laid waste to many parts of Northern England, especially Cheshire. Earl Edwin of Mercia and Chester held lands in Wirral, he and his followers rebelled against William's rule over England, this led William to punish the inhabitants by laying villages to waste throughout Cheshire and many areas of Northern England; not all England's populace wanted William for their King.

The Abbey in Chester was the only pre conquest land owner to keep their lands; in fact they were given many more great estates. The new landed gentry needed the church and its brethren to pray for them, so when their time came for them to enter the Kingdom of Heaven they could do so with a clear conscience.

Today Puddington is a quiet place, but Cheshire and Wirral's past nearly 500 years ago was noted for its lawlessness. In 1540 King Henry VIII ended the right of sanctuary, but in some of the Pallatine counties such as Cheshire they maintained sanctuary conditions.
Sanctuary was granted for all offences except murder, rape, robbery, sacrilege and housebreaking. Petty crimes in Wirral and Cheshire were rife.
The Earl of Chester for payments made, offered sanctuary for a year and a day in certain parts of the county, perhaps this was the reason for the high crime rate? To deal with the matter, local justices of the peace were appointed; they met four times a year in Chester.

William Massey was elected Sheriff in 1440 and 1437, and then in 1439 he was elected Major of Chester. The Massey family lived in Puddington.

In 1715 Sir William Massey, during the Civil war was a royalist and assisted in the defence of Chester.
Many families during the civil war were divided by their loyalties, either to the crown or to Oliver Cromwell. While Sir William was absent from Puddington, the roundheads burnt down part of his home.

After the battle of Preston, legend has it that Sir William Massey rode his horse from Preston back to Puddington, crossing the Mersey at low tide between Speke and Hooton, a distance of 45 miles. At 60 years old this was some feat. Did his zeal for home overcome the endurance of the ride? When he arrived at Puddington, his horse collapsed and died in the courtyard. William was captured and imprisoned in Chester Castle, where he died shortly after, having been found frozen to death in his cell.

Old Puddington Hall 2009

Roundhead troops are known to have been billeted at Puddington Hall.

There was a Deer park in Puddington Manor when Wirral was 'afforested', in which the Earls and Barons took to hunting; the field names give a clue as to the use of the land.

The Massey's of Puddington were a powerful family; in 1403 John Massey was killed at the Battle of Shrewsbury. [An interesting point concerning the church of St Mary Magdalene, it was erected on the site of the Battle of Shrewsbury 607 years ago]. The church is a lovely place to visit and very atmospheric. There is a booklet available in the church describing the events of the battle.

Richard Massey was the first to settle in Puddington in the 14th century, and Sir William was the last of the Massey family, the estate passed to his godson from the Stanley family.

Puddington is tucked away off the A540, it has no inn or post office, only pretty red sandstone and limewashed houses. There is a small triangular green bounded by a typically British red telephone kiosk and a penstock with apple trees and the obligatory sheep.

Puddington Old Hall was built in 1490, it had a Tudor timber frame structure with traces of an open gallery, and rectangular in form, which is all it has to show of its early history. There was a drawbridge, which was dismantled during the 1840s, and there are scant remains of a moat. From the footpath alongside the hall you can glimpse what remains of the moat.
The 1841 tithe map shows the moat being on three sides of the hall, two aligned north-south, and one aligned east-west.The hall also boasted of a Columbarium or Dovecot, of which there were only two in Wirral. 'A Dovecot provided fresh meat all year round'

There was a secret place within the chimney at Puddington Old Hall, it is where a priest named John Plessington hid from the puritans, and on the 19th July 1679 he was betrayed and captured. He was then hung, drawn and quartered at Gallows Hill, Alford in Chester, and his crime? He was a catholic priest.

His remains should have been displayed at Puddington to warn other would be royalists, but his family buried his remains at Burton graveyard.
In 1962 a grave was opened to try and identify the remains as that of John Plessington, but this could not be proved. John Plessington was canonised in 1970, 'St John Plessington Martyr 1637-79.'

In 1662 – 1688 a hearth tax was levied over the country. Puddington Old Hall was recorded as having twelve hearths, maybe not a cold and draughty place after all!

A new Puddington Hall was built in 1760, and is located on the left as you enter the village. There was a fire during Christmas 1867, and part of the house was destroyed. I wonder what happened to their Christmas dinner!

Burton church records show that a passenger from Ireland died in Puddington on xxxi *daie of March 1620.* Perhaps the passenger was visiting someone from the hall! Having the means to travel in those days was outside most ordinary folks' income.

A Walk around Puddington Village

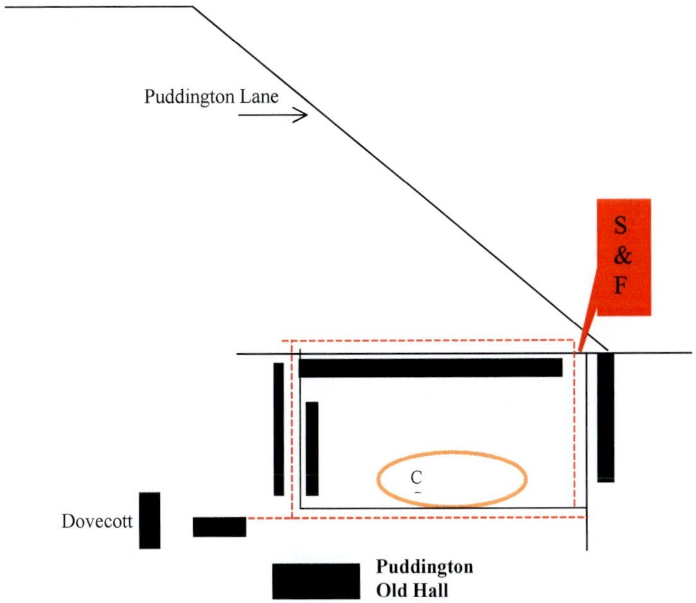

To walk around the village start at the telephone kiosk, opposite you will see a number of cottages, cross the road and turn left, you will reach the Old Forge cottage.

The Tithe map of 1841 lists the cottage and gardens as being occupied by John Edwards 'Smithy'. Stanley Cottage was occupied by the Stanley's in 1841. Turn right after Stanley Cottage onto a footpath, you will notice some large sandstone blocks as part of garden boundary walls, when you reach the bottom of the lane take the footpath on the right. This footpath or lane as it was in 1841, was known as Occupation Lane, it extended past the Old Hall and on towards the coast, it also went in the opposite direction nearly reaching what is now the A540.

Walk up the footpath within a few yards you will notice a lovely tranquil garden on your right, the sunlight and dappled shade enhancing the atmosphere of the garden. This area of land, mentioned in the tithes maps, was called the Croft and was owned by the Old Hall.

To the left of the footpath you can now catch a glimpse of Puddington Old Hall. It is just beyond the copse of sycamore trees. On an October day the ivy clad walls shimmer with a crimson glow as the rays of the sun are cast on its walls. There is an air of mystery here, glance around in search of the moat. Possibly the sunken ground on the left, where some trees have fallen, is all that remains of the moat.

Within a few yards you reach Old Hall Lane, turn right here. As you walk up the lane you will notice a number of the cottages here are named after flowering shrubs. At the top of the lane turn right and you are back at the start of your walk.

As you may have noticed, the village has a number of relatively old cottages and houses, which sit comfortably side by side with some quite modern buildings.

On the Tithe map of 1841 there were seven houses and nine cottages in the village, here are the names of a few occupants from that period.

Robert Mann
Thomas Hancock
Isaac Dean Jamieson
John William Maddocks
George Peers
Thomas Challoner
Elizabeth Jackson
Henry Gray
John Bell
Henry Heyes

Rev. Richard Gillow
Richard Foster
John Jones
Samuel Smith
John Williams
Richard Watkin
William Ollerhead
John Edwards
Richard Vanhegan

The house with a date plate of 1716 on the right of the village green was occupied by Henry Heyes in 1841.

This concludes are walk in Puddington, you may now travel to Burton by vehicle, or continue approximately one mile on the footpath.

Puddington to Burton a walk of 1 mile

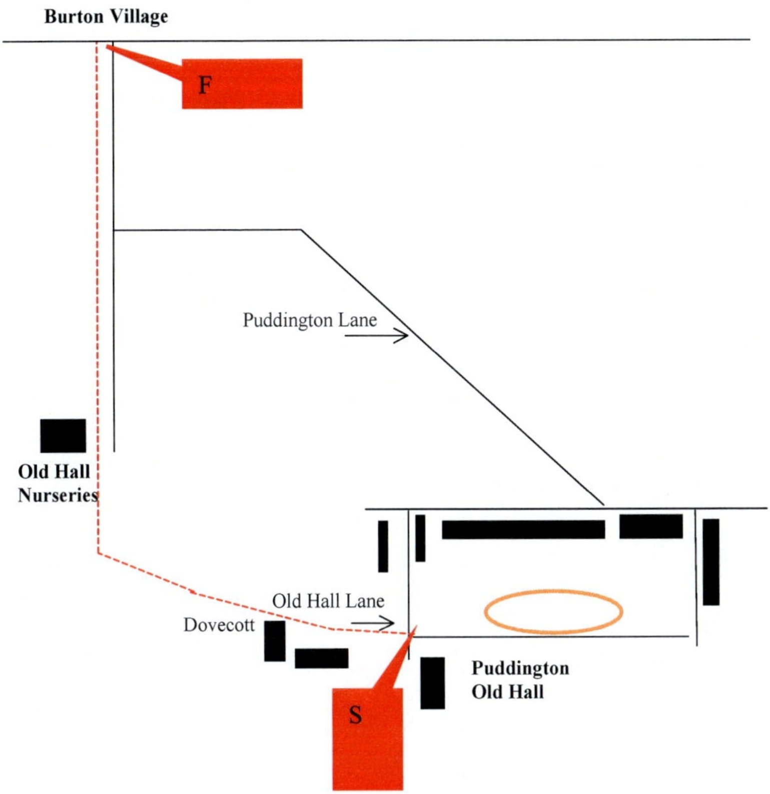

Chapter: 4 Puddington to Burton

It is 1 mile from Puddington to Burton. From the village green walk down Old Hall Lane, at the end of the lane is a footpath on the right. The footpath takes you past converted farm buildings which once belonged to the Old Hall, 'The Barns, Paddock, Stables and the Dovecot'. Just after the Dovecot is a hitch-hatch gate, go through and cross the open yard area and then through another hitch-hatch gate.

You are now on a metalled road. Once past the two houses on the left, you will notice a large stone wall on your left which leads to a small nursery called 'Old Hall Nurseries'. Interesting selections of shrubs are for sale at the nursery, the walls and building at the entrance show a glimpse into the past use of the buildings.

Once past the nursery there is a clear view of the estuary and its reclaimed land. No, you are not dreaming if you see boats in the distance, for the reclaimed land also boasts a boating lake. Continue on down to the end of the lane, on either side of the lane's abutment with Puddington Lane you will notice substantial boundary walls of red sandstone. Carry on down Puddington Lane, Burton's tithe barn is halfway along Puddington Lane, on the left. It is on private property.
On reaching a T junction you are now in Burton village.

Notes on Burton Village

The village of '*Burtone*'was recorded in error in the Doomsday book under '*The Rushton Hundred'* and not *'Willaston Hundred'*.
There was land for:
3 hides which paid geld
7 ploughs including 2 ploughs for the Desmense (for the use of the Lord of the manor)
7 Villeins
4 Bordars
1 Priest
1 Radman with 3 ploughs
There was also 1 acre of meadow; all of this was worth 40 shillings before 1066, and 15 shillings after 1066.

Burton's location for a village or fortified farmstead was not by accident; Burton's geographical location is situated on the south side of a 222 ft. ridge of high ground on a rocky plateau.

The village was screened from the north by tree clad hills, with its low lying ground towards the sea. It must have seemed an ideal place for Anglo-Saxons to settle at Burton Point in 900 A.D, what with its sheltered bay and boulder clay fields.

Burton was an agricultural community, few farms remain today, but it has kept its rural identity, not so for many other villages along the coast.
A pretty ribbon of road winds past sandstone cottages some perched atop on red sandstone crags. Burton village is a stone's throw from the old coastline, situated down a quiet country lane which deviates abruptly as you reach the salt marshes.

From the pre-conquest days until the 19th century the Bishop of Coventry and Lichfield were Lords of Burton Manor. In 1298 Edward I gave to the Bishop of Lichfield the right to hold a market and a three day annual fair, which was held in July before the feast of St James.

These village markets were the main stay of the area, and provided an exchange of goods local and foreign which the community could enjoy.
Sadly, no longer are markets and fairs a sight to see and enjoy in Burton.

Celia Fiennes visited Burton in 1695; she accomplished a grand tour of England riding side saddle. Celia wrote how she had travelled over the sands from Flint to Burton with two guides who knew the route well. They informed her that the route constantly changes due to the deposits of sand across the estuary. Celia then travelled to Liverpool from Burton; it took one and a half hours on the ferry to cross the River Mersey.

The name '*Burton* 'is generally meant to mean *'burgh'* meaning earthwork and *'ton'* a fortified homestead or headland, from which Burton Point received its Anglo-Saxon name.

Burton Village, Wood, Mill and Well 1¼ miles

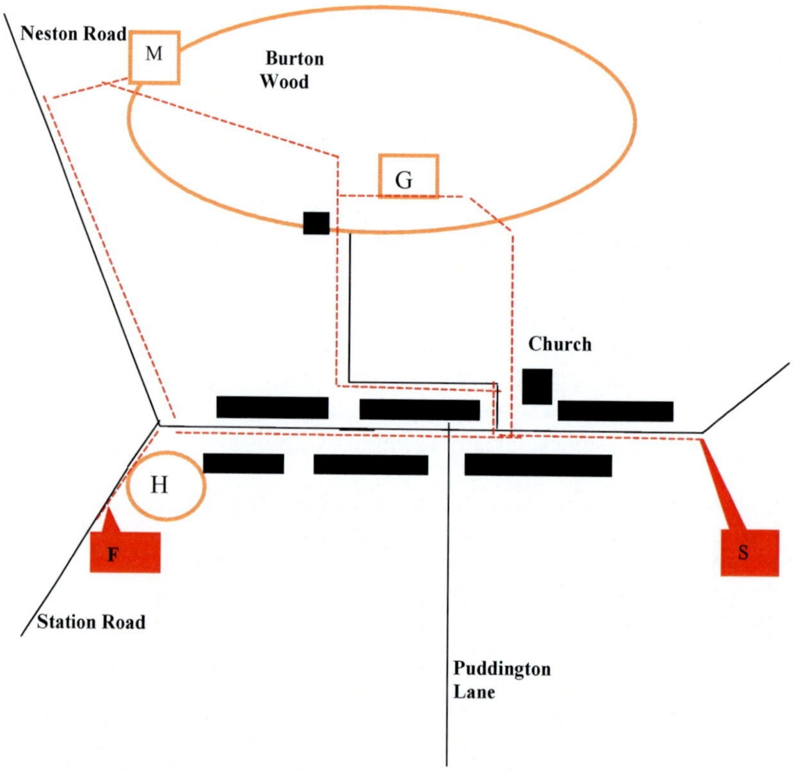

M= site of Burton Mill
G= site of Quakers Grave
H= site of Hampston Well

Chapter 5: Burton Village

To start the walk begin on the east side of the Village, the road here has no footpath so take care, on both sides of the road you will notice red sandstone bedrock jutting up from the ground, enticing you to stop and observe its heavily pebbled surface. Walk east to west through the village, at sunset the sandstone rocks from which the houses seem to organically sprout, are cast in a fiery glow; in fact it's quite difficult to walk west without shading your eyes from the sun's rays.

On your right you soon reach Vicarage Lane, where up on a grassy mound stands a sandstone cross. It is called a Holy Cross and was erected on September 14th 1917; it was donated by a lady of the village who felt compelled to commemorate the dead after hearing of the battle of the Somme.

There is a footpath here which leads to Neston up through Burton Wood, 20 acres of woodland was given to the National Trust in 1928 by the Bulley family of Ness. Predominantly these were pine woods, were once home to the red squirrel, but only the grey squirrels have their home here now. Areas like this across Britain are held in trust for everyone to enjoy.

The two cottages on your right are where the Smithy and Smithy croft stood in 1848.

Carry on walking on the road, take care - traffic and no pavement! To the left and right stand more pretty cottages: Tithe cottage, Rock cottage, Ivy Bank all are elevated from the road.

On your left is the Village hall, it was founded on behalf of the brave men of Burton who left their homes to fight in the 1914-1918 war, sadly many never returned.

The wood on the right teeters on the edge of the road only to retreat behind the Church in a few more yards, there is a gate to the Church here but for now carry straight on.'Church Farm House' stands on the left of the road and has a date stone of 1678; adjacent is 'The Bawns Cottages' both modernised over the years.

Puddington Lane is on the left, to the right a small lane leads up to the Church, here is Pear Tree cottage with a date stone of 1682 and initials JL + SL - this was John Leather and Sarah Brown who married in Chester on 14th August 1657, they had a son born in 1661 called Thomas.

Turn right onto the little lane, the Church beckons to the right, and an interesting lane emerges on the left.

Let's take the lane on the left for now; on the Tithe map of 1848 the lane runs behind the cottages which face the main road, in 1848 the rear gardens of these crofts are where the new houses on the right are.

The' Rake' Burton 2010

The 'Rake' is a sunken lane which runs downhill; turn right. As you walk up the lane you reach Rake Cottage on the left.

Climb the stone steps and turn right at the footpath sign into Burton wood. At the time of writing there were hundreds of conkers strewn over the ground, don't children play conkers anymore?

The footpath climbs slowly up through the wood, travelling eastward, in a few minutes you will come across an unusual sight; Quakers graves.

Quakers Grave in Burton Wood

The graves are believed to be man and wife who were buried in this unconsecrated spot because Quakerism was thought at the time to be evil. The grave stones are no longer readable but a sign states

'The body of ELL and 7 I N I '

It has been quoted that they may have been buried in an upright position.

There is a plaque at the grave site commemorating: '*courageous men and women in difficult times'*, the dedications were from the year 1938 and 1980. 344 years have passed; their graves are still outside of the Church grounds, so spare a thought for them as you pass by.

A little further on take the path to the right, then down some old sandstone steps and into the churchyard.

Let's spend some time here at St Nicholas Church. In 1086 the first church was made of wood , a stone church was built in the 12th century, then in 1380 another church was built; little is known of either of these churches, except for the following antiquities found:

Norman scalloped capitals where found buried in the churchyard, now they rest in the porch of the church. Over the entrance to the Church you will notice engravings by the stone masons and carpenters who all took a pride in their work.
The base of the inner wall by the Massey chapel and a 14th century window is all that remains of the earlier Church.
Inside the porch is a 13th century stone coffin lid, at the altar there is a Jacobean communion rail, and the chair behind the rail dates back to King Charles II.

St Nicholas is the patron saint of mariners, so it would be fitting to have a church so near the sea dedicated to him. A legend referring to St Nicholas says that a poor man had three daughters, each wanting to marry, for marriages to take place a dowry had to be paid by the father of the bride.
'The father had no money for any of his daughters to marry so St Nicholas gave him three bags of gold to pay for each of his daughters weddings'.
You will notice carved on the lectern, three moneybags associated with the legend. A pamphlet from the church, describes in detail the churches history.

The parish registers and papers at one time were always kept in the 'Parish Chest', these papers tell the history of a village or town. The parish register starts from 1538 and lists the vicars of Burton dating back to Simon de Sachell in 1302, and included in these registers are references to the plague which struck Burton and neighbouring villages in Wirral.

The steeple was pointed in 1617 *'by men of Liverpool at Bartholomew tyde'*

Simple entries such as;
Oct 1665, *five girls of the 'Dutchman' died and where buried, their ages were one, twelve, fifteen, and nineteen, the last age is unclear.*
Dec 1665, *the plague ceased thanks be unto God.*

A memorandum in the Church wardens accounts:
'That there hath not been anything written in this register from yeare of 1646 untill the yeare of 1655 except 5 names, that are registered before by resun this register was out of the way and could not be found'.

Mistakes can happen anywhere, but a nine year gap can mean a great deal to a family historian.

The last entry in the register for 1646 was by Rector Henry Trafford stating: *funerals were to take place between the hours of 4 and 5 after the noon in August before the feast of St Bartholomew'*
Apart from complete omissions, other errors are found:
In 1835 William Perry married Isabella Briggs on the 8th May, inconsistencies in the use of the registers showed the vicar had placed the marriage on page five of the registers in the year 1819!

Further entries record news bulletins such as:
1645, September 20th. *Parliament forces entered Chester Forgatt Streete fired.*
1645, September 24th. A *terrible battle on Rowton Moor and Hoole Heath.*
1660, *King Charles II of England Scotland Ireland was proclaimed the Fifteenth day of May Who God long preserve.*

The minutes in the churchwarden's accounts where required to be 'Announced' every Sunday to the congregation. This was at the time the local news media! As too was bell ringing, in 1780, 3s8d was paid to bell ringers for ringing good news, I wonder what price bad news!

Let's take a walk outside in the churchyard, the red sandstone walls of the church stand proud against the tree crowned summit of Burton wood. The church clock has only one hand, labour on the land many years ago required you only needed to know the hour of the day and not the minutes. The sundial is from the 18th century and stands to the south of the church.

Churches have always played a prominent role in any village and therefore the upkeep of the church was critical. Tithes were paid for the upkeep of the church and its clergy; as far back as 1494 Tithes for Burton and Denhall Hospital were received.
In England and Wales over 11,800 Tithe surveys were made mostly before 1841, they finished in 1851.
In Cheshire 91% of the land was covered by the surveys.
A Tithe was represented as a 1/10th of the annual increase of the produce of the soil, it was paid to the rector or incumbent of the parish, and was payable on;
1 Fruits of the earth; crops.
2 Animal products; colts – lambs – wool – milk - eggs
3 Personal; which was profits from milling or fishing, generally meant the profit on a man's labour.
Tithe produce was then collected and usually placed in a Tithe barn to be dealt with accordingly.

While we linger in the churchyard you will see that some gravestones show the tragic reminders of times past; there is an obelisk to the west of the church entrance commemorating the deaths of the children of George and Mary Day.
Four sons drowned together in a pond in Puddington they were buried on 4th March 1888. They were:
Charles 17
John 14
William 8
George (?)
What a tragedy to befall any family, the inhabitants of Burton were so moved by this tragedy that they collected funds to provide a fitting headstone for the grief stricken parents.

Another sad reminder of village life; Sarah Hughes buried 6 children aged from 18 months to 6 years, four of these children died within the same year 1842, she herself died aged 55 in 1864.

Life was very hard then and child mortality high, as can be witnessed on many other gravestones. You will notice a number of grave slabs perched on round sandstone blocks at the rear of the church; they are mostly illegible now due to the horizontal position of the grave slabs.

On one visit to the church, the church bells were rung, this reminded me of a note I had read in the church warden's accounts:
In 1780 the bells were rung when Charlestown was captured by Cornwallis in the Americas, the payment for ringing the bells was 3s.8d.

On leaving the Church go out through the gate and turn left, past Pear Tree cottage and onto the main road. Turn right and walk up the road, Rose Cottage is on your right a lovely black and white timber building.
The Old Post Office is on the right with St Nicholas house on the left.

Church House is another black and white timber building with crooked walls and various floor levels and windows.

On the right is a lovely thatched house called Barn End, it is raised up on the natural red sandstone bedrock, the footpath here joins the path you took earlier, up into Burton wood.

As you continue up the main road, just before you reach Burton Manor is Rake Farm cottage, you will notice a doorway or hatch bricked up low down to the right of the building, possibly a cellar entrance, there is also a mullioned window which has been sealed. A little further round the bend in the road opposite Burton Manor is Bishop Wilson's birthplace. It is a lovely thatched cottage, Bishop Wilson was born here in 1663, later he became the 'Bishop of Sodor and Man' (Isle of Man). He founded a school here in 1724 for the children of the parish; the original school building is now a private house.

As you have seen there are many fine houses here today, in 1663 Burton was listed as paying Hearth Tax on the following homes:
35 houses where taxed with 1 hearth.
3 houses with 2 hearths
1 house had 7 hearths. This was a large house by any standards.

Opposite is Burton Manor, now an adult education college. It was once the residence of the Congreve family; you may have noticed many gravestones in the churchyard with this name. The manor was built in 1805 by the Congreve family and rebuilt in 1904, an exceptional note worth recording of this family; is that two family members won the Victoria Cross. Captain Walter Norris Congreve 1862-1927 won the Victoria Cross in South Africa in 1899, his son William La Touche Congreve was posthumously awarded a Victoria Cross in July 1916, one of only three father and sons to be awarded Britain's highest award for bravery.

Chapter 6: To the Site of Burton Mill

A view of Burton Mill in the late 1800s by kind permission of Neston Library

There is no longer a mill in Burton; photographs are now the only visual record of the mill. The walk up the hill to the site of the old mill is a pleasant stroll of ½ mile.
Walk up the road towards Ness past the 'Y' junction with Station Road, Mill Lane is on the right, walk up the lane, sandstone bedrock and large sandstone walls mark the boundaries of this lane. Where the lane turns left there is a Hitch Hatch gate and old sandstone steps on the right, these lead you back into the woods but for now stay on the road.

On the right is Old Mill House as the sign in the garden demonstrates. Pause awhile and read the name on the old sandstone gate pillars 'Mill Cottage', it denotes an older building but first impressions suggest a fairly new house.
At the top of the lane is a house called Mill Wood, on the right nearly hidden by shrubs is a footpath, take the footpath for a few yards and it leads past the rear of Old Mill House, here you will notice the older Mill Cottage, a lovely red sandstone property.

It's a pity that the mill is no longer there, records for this site go back as far as 1298. In 1579 John Haggassman the Miller '*was killed by a thunder bolt'.*
Sir William Massey built a mill at the time of the feast of All Saints in 1629. Edward Sumner was a miller at Burton, he died in 1629. The mills that once stood here where called 'Peg Mills' as you may determine from the photograph, the mill was known locally as Bobbin Mill. The Mill was finally destroyed by a gale in 1882.

Now retrace your steps back to the hitch hatch gate, enter the wood, the path on the right leads down to the main road, the path on the left leads to the summit of Burton Wood, keep to the path which leads straight ahead. It's a pleasant walk taking only a few minutes, a glimpse of the estuary emerges through the trees of pine, beech, holly, horse chestnut and oak.

Walk straight on keeping the boundary fence and walls on your right, the trees here are of considerable age. With many hollows in the ground collecting water coupled with fallen leaves, a mini bog has been created! On reaching a small clearing a shelter of logs and bracken has been constructed, someone has been watching Ray Mears and his survival techniques!

Still keeping the boundary on your right, the path continues up and down the hillocks and eventually meets the footpath which begins at Rake Cottage, turn right and walk down the sunken lane which leads back to the main road.

Chapter 7: To Burton Well

Burton's Well, pictured in the late 1800s
By kind permission from Neston Library

The walk to Burton Well from the village is ½ mile, the well or natural spring being located outside the village on the road to Burton Point. As you leave the village where the road forks, turn left into Station Road, within a few hundred yards on the left is a copse of trees behind a clearing, to the foreground is 'Hampston's well' Burton Well.

It was restored in 1975 by Ellesmere Port borough council as a tribute to Horace Edger Green who died aged 86 in 1973. There is a plaque commemorating this event, which includes the history of the well, and is set on a pair of 'sandstone rollers'.

The well is described as possibly serving the Iron-Age settlement at Burton Point, and in 900 A.D the Anglo-Saxon settlement at Burton. The earliest records of a well are first recorded in the Manor Court book in 1602 and 1603, the well was then known as Patrick's well.

The Manor Court records state that constables were charged to keep the well clean on a yearly basis, if not they were fined 6d, funds were also raised for maintaining the well. Punishment was wielded to anyone caught washing their clothes in it! During the 19th century the well became known as Hampston's well after a local family of that name.

In 1848 the Tithe map showed five fields to the south and south west of Burton Point with the names 'Well Crofts and Well Field', which showed their close proximity to Burton well.

There is no longer a pump at the well to draw up water, but above the photograph depicts how it used to look. To take a closer look; walk past the inscribed plaque, to the right you will notice a small path in the grass which leads down the slope towards the well or spring within the bounds of what seems a lost garden! The well is not brick built, but a natural spring bringing forth water deep from beneath the sandstone bedrock.

The area is overgrown now, nettles and weeds compete to cover the stone steps and flag stones, the spring is circular in shape with a rivulet of water trickling off towards Burton Point. The Ordnance Survey map marks the beginning of a stream on the map at this point.

It's a quiet place, birds sit aloft in a garden of trees - fir, willow, holly, sycamore and horse chestnut.

Stolen views of the estuary can be picked out between the trees, as I gaze on the view my mind ponders on what conversations took place here over the many hundreds of years when the well had provided water for the local inhabitants. Perhaps they spoke of crops, children, the weather, church, death, visitors or even invaders. Perhaps not so far removed from today's topics I would imagine.

Chapter 8: To Burton Point 1 ¼ miles

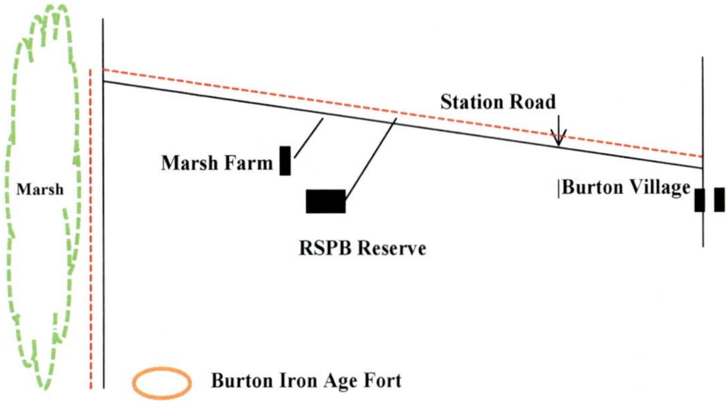

The walk is a distance of 1¼ miles from Burton village. When walking or driving down Station Road to Burton Point, proceed with caution the road is narrow and there are no footpaths.

The land is elevated at this point, as you continue down along the lane towards the estuary. '*Good land resting on clay'* was recorded in 1849 in 'The Farmers Club.' Field names in the area are recorded as Well Crofts, Holland Side, Little Holland, Far Rock Field, Near Rock Field and Field next to Rock Field; I think they ran out of names!

At the bottom of Station Road the marsh spreads out before you. If travelling by car park your vehicle on the side of the road alongside the marsh, go through the curved metal gate and walk up the tarmac road, in ¾ mile you will reach Burton Point.

The sandstone cliffs have been quarried for its fine red sandstone, the cliffs at one time extended much further out into what is now marsh.

Past the sheep pen on the right and within a few yards the road finishes, glance over to the left, on the hill stands Burton Promontory Iron Age Fort; as yet there is no access to the 'Fort'.

The marsh here is left undisturbed and it is home to thousands of breeding birds. The RSPB purchased 75 acres of abandoned arable land and Inner Marsh Farm in 1986, then in 1988 Burton Point Farm was purchased, the reserve was opened in 1992. Many hundreds of acres of marsh now owned by the RSPB have been awarded 'Special Site of Scientific Interest'.

Twelve water buffalos were originally introduced to create muddy hollows for nesting lapwings, but when Shotton Steel industry ceased drilling bore holes to extract water from the marsh the water table rose therefore becoming too wet for even the water buffalo.

There are now reed beds, lakes and acres of wet land for a huge variety of birds that visit the area every year. Opposite are the reed beds at Burton Point pictured in 2009.

Burton Iron Age Fort 2008

The Iron Age Fort is a scheduled 'ancient monument' at Burton Point and is on land belonging to the RSPB, Colin Wells, the site manager, gave me permission to photograph the area. On a cold wet November day warden Stuart Taylor walked me to the 'Fort'. It is an amazing place, Burton Point juts out into the estuary, and views on all sides are unrestricted when standing atop the 20 metre contour line.

There are no obvious ancient plough marks in the ground, only slight undulations can be observed. To the left of the high ground, on the Point, there is a small copse of trees, now in winter they are denuded of their leaves, showing the Iron Age Fort at its best.
The high ground looking down shows the mound and part of the ditch quite clearly, it stands near the edge of the 10 metre contour line, and certainly provided its occupants with an excellent vantage point with commanding views up and down the estuary.

The Iron Age Fort is a promontory fort and dates from the 6th century BC to 1st century AD; it is the only one of this type in England, but is typical of those found in North Wales and the Isle of Man. They are regarded as being of high status settlements, and where occupied on a permanent basis.
The Fort is stated as being '*A 60 metre long arc shaped defensive bank on 1 side retaining a height of 3.5 metres above the ditch and 2.5 metres internal ground surface'*.

Walking alongside the 'fort' it forms two mounds with the ditch running between them. Nearing the southern boundary of the mound there is a track which leads down towards what was once the shore line, the track is steep with grass and moss now covering the sandstone bedrock.

Nearing the bottom of the path the ground opens out onto flat marsh, the high sandstone cliffs coloured red and pink with black water marks running down to the ground stand proud before you. Owls and Kestrels use the cliffs as a vantage point for hunting.

The cliffs have been heavily quarried, part of the north and south outer defences of the Fort have been lost.The flat area opposite the cliffs where the stream runs was once the port of Burton; it's still a sheltered place and would have provided a safe haven for ships anchoring on the leeward side of Burton Point, even before quarrying reduced the extent of the cliff line.

In 1399 archers went to Ireland to fight with King Richard. Burton was known as an outlying Port for Chester. In the 15th century it was an international port where Spanish vessels brought wine, cloves, cork, sugar, exotic goods and raisins destined for the wealthy.

Burton Point stretched further out into the estuary than it does today. The sandstone cliffs here have been quarried for building stone used for sea defences and stones for Flint Castle!
The stratification on the sandstone cliffs shows the uplift and overlying of rocks as the land was formed over 208 million years ago.

On the seaward side of the cliffs there are tidal defences 'Dykes' that stretch for nearly 3 miles towards Shotton and Connahs Quay. In the 18th century the tidal defences were breeched, but today they mark a route on a map with no public access, save for the 1500 sheep who are brought onto the marsh daily by a shepherd called Andrew who comes from Northumberland.

On a late November afternoon geese, fowl and moorhen are my companions, the sky suddenly darkening as hundreds of birds fly in like a swarm of bees, coming to rest on the inner marsh. It's a beautiful place and the RSPB since 2009 have provided the access which you are now enjoying as you walk to Burton Point.

Burton church records reveal, in August 1637 a statement from William Farrar said '*an internment of 41 had occurred'*. It is not known who these people were, it has been said they most likely were from a shipwreck and perhaps of Irish decent. It has been recorded that *Irish men were of larger stature than Englishmen'.*

In 1878 a number of skeletons were found buried on the point *'50 to 60 coffined men of large stature'* P Sully states*: 29 were laid east to west and no weapons or grave goods were found.*

Denhall Quay and Ness a 1¼ mile walk

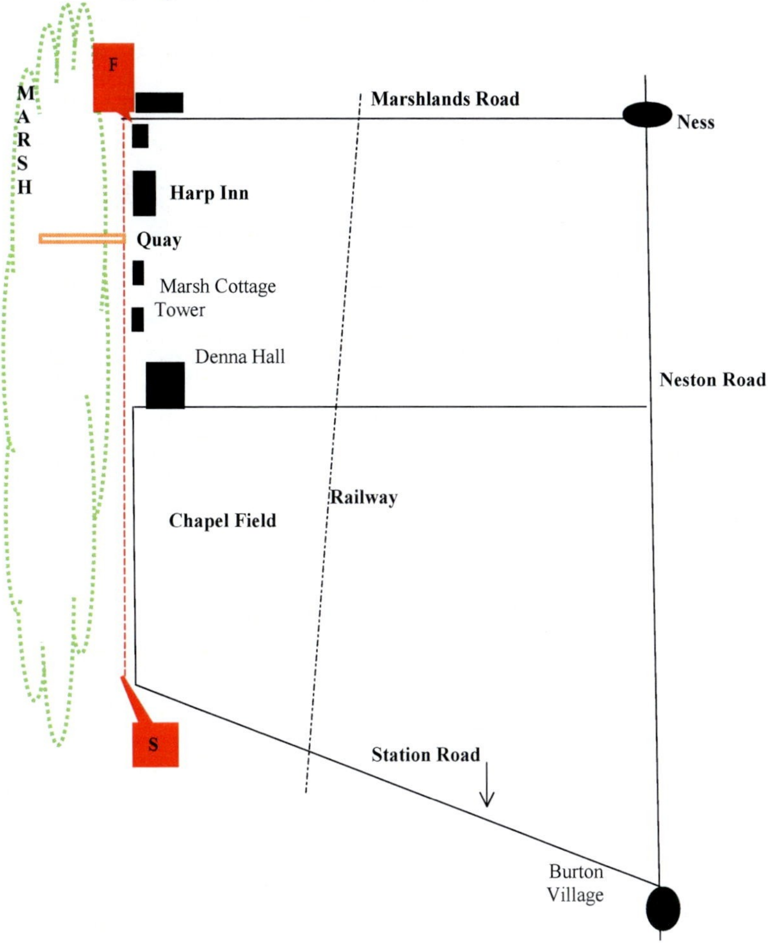

Chapter 9: To Denhall Quay and Ness

The walk to Denhall and Ness is 1¼ miles. From Station Road north west of Burton, the walk starts from the parking area on the edge of the marsh.
The marsh to your left out towards Sealand is sometimes used as a firing range and at certain times a red flag flies warning you of the danger.
This area abounds with ancient history but little of it can be seen, but when you are aware of its past a whole new picture unfolds.

View of Chapel Field, site of 'The Hospital of St Andrew' 2008

On your right is a sandstone wall, beyond is 'Chapel Field' in the south east rises a spring from which the area takes its name '*Danewell'*, its Old Norse and means Danes Spring of which this is the only one so named in Wirral.
Here in Chapel Field in 1231 – 1234 the hospital of St Andrew was built for the '*help of the poor, shipwrecked, and travellers to and from Ireland'*. The hospital was built on a west facing slope a short distance from the shoreline, the precinct wall of the hospital lies on the fields western boundary and still forms part of the boundary wall.

There are numerous banks of earth which cover the remains of the hospital buildings. The Chapel is sited on the old cliff line (10 metre contour) which can be seen as a steady rise in the ground towards the south east. Also to be found on the cliff line are the remains of a post medieval limekiln, in the form of a bank 0.7metre high which forms a circle about 5 metres in diameter.

This whole area became a scheduled monument in 1975, and in 1999 a new archaeological ground survey was completed defining the following areas of the hospital: chapel, infirmary, drainage systems and further outbuildings.

In addition a track way running through the middle of the site was identified, including the perimeter wall of the hospital precinct. It was recorded that the track probably led to what was the site of medieval quays across the mouth of the inlet, quite possibly for loading and unloading cargo anchored in the Dee estuary.

The hospital was built by Alexander Stavensby Bishop of Coventry and Lichfield, and it was annexed to Burton church. In 1251 the Pope confirmed liberties and privileges to the prior and its brethren and sisters. It was a mixed community and so confirmed by a land grant made by the prior. The hospital was never a wealthy one and was only valued at £10 a year in 1300s. Privileges were given to the prior and the hospital these were:
Fishing rights in the River Dee, the right of wreck, free warren of rabbits on the lands of the hospital.
Boats were not allowed to anchor without the master's permission.
Tolls were claimed on goods landed there for transport to Chester by land or sea. The masters of the hospital did not need a licence to buy goods from Chester, they were free from tolls, and the Sheriff and other officials could not enter land or water of the hospital without permission!

Even with these privileges the hospital still struggled to survive. Sadly with its decline in 1496 the hospital became too impoverished to continue independently.
In 1675 Francis Ashenhurst settled the site on his future wife, and it stayed in the family until 1738 when it was partly demolished with the permission of the Bishop, Master of St John. In 1751 the remains of the hospital were demolished except for one converted barn; in 1897 some remains were still visible.

This apparently empty field was witness to a life of hope for the poor and shipwrecked, business and commerce for the city of Chester, and a chosen way of life for the brethren and sisters who lived here. To finally become mounds in a grassy field with no outward signs of life is rather sad. A sign acknowledging the history of the hospital would be an advantage to all!

Walk on down the lane with the shoreline on your left, at the road junction Denhall Lane turns right uphill, we take the footpath leading us straight ahead. Notice on your left a rusty signpost, look on the rear of the sign, it reads; *'John Summer and Son's. Private Road, Denhall Farm and Denna Farm only'.*

Don't worry this is a right of way for pedestrians only. Denna Hall was built in 1831; it's now a listed building, the main entrance being on Denhall Lane.
In 1865 an addition to the porch was made incorporating older stonework, which, quite possibly, came from the hospital of St Andrew. Denna Hall was once a nursing home but is now a private residence.

Richard Summer bought a property here on the Wirral in 1925 for £10,000; he had a road built across the marsh to John Summers Steel Works. Roundabouts were placed at each end of the road allowing him to race his cars; he was a keen car enthusiast. As a point of interest, John Summers Steel Works which is based in Shotton, helped the war effort during World War Two by producing Anderson air raid shelters, millions of Jerri cans, petrol cans and millions of tons of metal sheet. Sir Richard Summer was knighted in 1963 for services to the steel industry; he died in 1977.

The western boundary of Denna Hall is a high sandstone wall covered with ivy, it prevents any view of the hall except for its chimney pots, I counted 40!
As you walk along the footpath you will notice the remains of two white doors built into the sandstone wall, which are now partially covered by ivy.
Hidden doors, overgrown ivy, secret gardens; reminds me of a book I loved as a child 'The Secret Garden'.

The end of the wall terminates at a rectangular sandstone tower, complete with coloured glass windows covered with wire mesh and overgrown by ivy. An attempt to remove the ivy had begun at the time of writing. The tower has not yet been dated and may have been a folly.

The Tower in the grounds of Denna Hall 2008

Next to the tower is Marsh Cottage, a pretty red brick building, the land here is at sea level. As you walk past Denhall Farm the land rises quite quickly and reaches the 10m contour. On the corner of a small lane abutting with the path, a World War Two bunker for sea defences sits above the footpath.

The abundance of bird life is a delight to see, particularly the short eared owls; the marsh is classed as a place of Scientific Interest.
Just after Denhall Farm on the left is a stile which gives access to the marsh, look out for the red flag.
The high ground to the right is the old cliff line where the tide would have ebbed and flowed, now only grass grows.
The footpath is now on an incline, a stone wall is on the right, and then a few feet further on the path joins another footpath from Neston.

Now on a tarmac road we come to the cottage Quay Stones, walk on past, within a few yards you reach a grassy promontory jutting out into the marsh this is Denhall Quay.

Denhall Quay2008

Interesting facts from Denhall:

In 1315 Stephen Gofry fled justice, his goods and properties were seized after he had murdered Bertram the miller of Denhall.

In 1689 Captain Greenville Collins produced a map of the Wirral coast, it recorded Denhall was a safe anchorage.

The promontory on which you are standing leads onto a pier which was built in 1791. It was built to help load coal into 'colliers', shallow drafted boats which could get up close to the quay. Ships from Denhall and Ness voyaged to Ireland, North Wales, Isle of Man, Spain and France.

The continuous silting of the Dee estuary was proving even more difficult for larger ships to reach the ports further downstream on the Dee. By 1737 the 'New Cut' was made in the River Dee's course, instead of hugging the Wirral coast it was now directed to the Welsh bank of the river.
This 'cut 'enabled a minimum depth of 16ft to be maintained in the channel, allowing once again larger ships to reach the City of Chester, but even this eventually was not enough for the port of Chester to continue. The changes to the course of the River Dee proved the death knell for the Wirral ports; it quickened the silting on its shoreline.

Here in 1759 Ness colliery was opened by Sir Thomas Stanley Baronet; he brought miners from Lancashire and North Wales to work in the mines.
The geological name for the area is the 'Wirral Colliery Fault', the coal seams being difficult to locate due to the faulting of the carboniferous beds which run out under the River Dee to Flint in North Wales.
The villages of Ness, Little Neston and Neston all stand on Triassic sandstone.

Pit heads at Denhall 1790 with kind permission From Neston Library

The coal pits that were dug here were quite shallow; having galleries 180ft to 282ft below the surface, all of these shafts ran out under the River Dee.
The entrances to some of these pits were only 200 yards from the high water mark. It was a dirty and hazardous job for man and boy.

Miners received a pittance in pay; their homes were stark with no running water. The underground galleries where they worked were reached by small canal barges, and then when loaded with coal, and with the men lying on their backs they used their feet to push the boat along by 'treading the gallery roof', which was very similar to the method used in Speedwell Cavern in Derbyshire.
Coal was put into baskets at the coal face and then placed on to barges for the return trip to the pit shaft. This method ceased in 1821. Some pit shafts were only about 2 metres in diameter; all of the shafts have now been capped to ensure safety. In 1830 only one pit was left open in Little Neston and six in Ness.

In 1841 the census recorded 27 miners living in the area.
In1850 the Denhall Gutter silted up.
In 1851 Denhall colliery re-opened after closure, but not for long, it proved too costly with only low grade coal being found.
In 1894 the ordnance survey map shows Denhall colliery disused. Further pits in Neston, worked by the Wirral Colliery, remained open and in 1920 employed 200/250 workers.

Anthony Annakin-Smith has written a detailed account of the mines and the miners who worked in them; it is available to read at Neston library.
The Port of Denhall had been a prosperous one in the past, but like many ports here on the River Dee, very soon went into decline due to the constant retreat of the waters, and the encroaching grasses of the marsh.
The first steam engine in Wirral was sited at Denhall; the great engineer George Stephenson visited the colliery. Denhall was the largest industrial site in the area.

Tithe maps of 1848 make reference to field names such as; Denhall hay, Denhall vetches, and Denhall fallow; these seem to refer to the methods of crop rotation.

Just before we leave Denhall, it is interesting to note that during an archaeological dig in Irby by Robert A. Philpot of the National Museums Liverpool, *'coal was found in a Smithying hearth, a sample of this coal and one from the coal spoil heaps at Denhall were sent for analysis and the two were found to be from the same locality.'* Perhaps coal from the Denhall area may have been used by Celts, Romans and Vikings!

Harp Inn 2011

A few yards on from the quay at Denhall you reach the Harp Inn, a good place to stop for light refreshment. It has unparalleled views of the River Dee.

Notes on NESS

The name 'Ness' is thought to be 'Old Norse' meaning promontory.
A Scandinavian settlement started in Wirral between 902 – 1014 AD.
Ness was recorded in the doomsday book in 1086, *Walter DeVernon held Ness from Earngeat who held it before him.*
There were 1½ hides paying geld and land enough for 2 ploughs.
In Desmense there was 1 plough
2 Oxmen
5 villeins
3 bordars with 2 ploughs
Including ½ acre of meadow, the whole was originally valued before the conquest at 20 shillings, after its value was 16 shillings.

Ness appeared to have been relatively spared the harrying by William the Conqueror compared to Little Neston!

Ness was the birth place of Emma Lyon christened Amy, 16th April 1765, known to all as Lady Hamilton, mistress of Lord Nelson. Emma was the eldest daughter of the local blacksmith who died when she was a baby, her mother returned to her home in Hawarden were Emma grew up.
Amy 'Emma' Lyon married William Hamilton; he was Britain's Ambassador to Naples.

Emma became Admiral Lord Nelson's mistress; she bore his children alone and in secret. When Nelson died she received no annuity from Britain and fled to Calais to escape the debtors' prison. Emma Hamilton died in Calais in poverty in 1813; she was buried in Eglise de St Pierre cemetery. During the rebuilding of Calais after World War Two the grave was lost.

Ness is famous for its botanical gardens, it was originally the home of Arthur Kilpin Bulley, and is located at Mickwell Brow in Ness. A hobby and an interest in plants soon saw the gardens filling with new species of which had been sourced from around the globe.
This hobby developed into a commercial nursery named 'Bee's Seeds'. Arthur Kilpin Bulley died in 1942; his daughter donated the gardens to the University of Liverpool three years later..

Ness Gardens are located on Burton Road, and are a must to visit at any time of the year, the views are stunning and there is plenty of space just to sit and soak up the peace and solitude. View their website for visiting times and forth coming events. 2011 was the 150th anniversary of the birth of the gardens creator, Arthur Kilpin Bulley.

Ness has also been the lure of the metal detectorist. In 1995, in a secret location, a silver ingot was found, it's now in the Liverpool Museum. The ingot was 46mm x 8mm x 9mm. As part of their manufacture, ingots would have been cast in an open mould of clay or stone, ingots could be easily carried and stored in this style, and the weight of the ingot was comparable with other Viking weight standards in Britain and Scandinavia from the 9th and 10th century.

One wonders whether the ingot was lost, or perhaps hidden to collect when danger had passed, but that day never came. There were no other finds made where the ingot was discovered.

The Harp Inn was previously named the Welch Harp; it's a nice place to rest awhile. Local miners regularly frequented the inn; they lived just a few yards away in New Street and Seven Row just off Marshlands Road.

Now that you are refreshed, walk towards the bottom of Marshlands Road, the house on your right in 1837 belonged to John Scott. The tithe maps of 1837 -54 shows that 1443 acres of *waste sands* in this area was owned by Rowland Errington!

Denhall to Neston Village

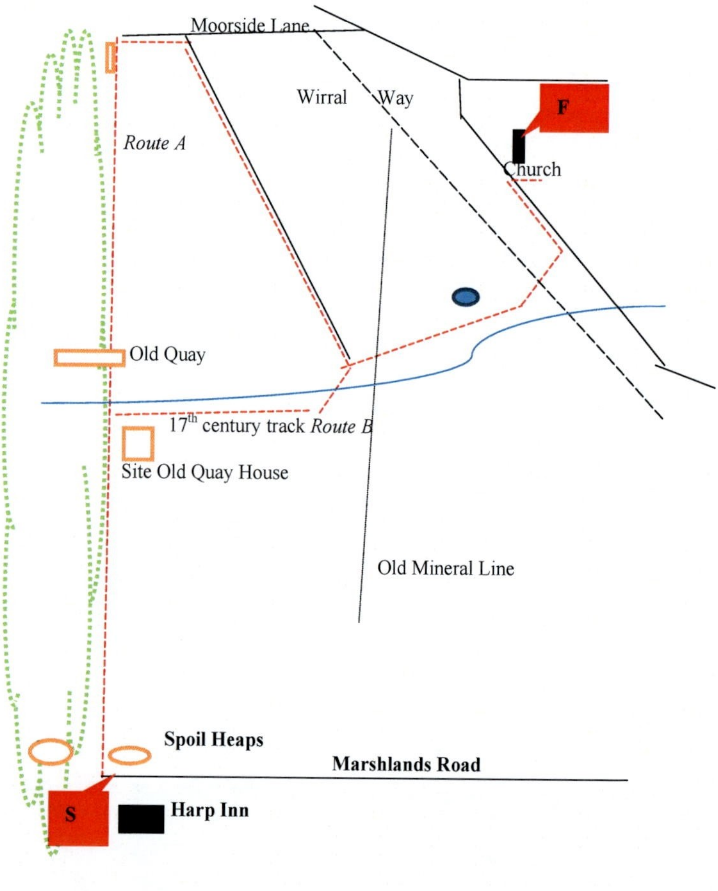

Chapter 10: Denhall to Neston

The walk continues along the coast towards Neston. Just a few yards past Marshlands Road you will notice small mounds on your left and large hillocks on your right, these are the remains of the spoil heaps from the coal mining industry. The spoil heaps have been landscaped to develop the area as an attraction for visitors and local inhabitants.

There is a good path for walking, the reed beds on your left stand tall and erect softly blowing in the breeze, in winter they are tinged with a golden hue, the view the miners had was not so pretty.

The path carries on northward, a small wall capped with sandstone on the right is reached, and reed beds give way to open marsh with the waters of the River Dee sparkling in the distance. It's very quiet here, birds are numerous, an ideal spot for bird watchers, and for us too!
Ahead, just at the top of a rise, two large sandstone gate pillars come into view, then on your right two smaller gate posts sited just in front of brambles and undergrowth.

Site of Old Quay house 2009

This is the site of the 'Old Quay House'; it was built circa 1600s as an Inn. During 1750 it became a 'house of correction to house Irish vagrants en route back to Ireland'. 25,000 vagrants passed through here between the years 1750 – 1800!

In 1758 between September 26th and 28th, the following people were deported back to Ireland from the New Quay:
Barnaby Sharp
Thomas Ryan
William Murphy
These were but a few, together with their families, they were returned to Ireland, at a cost of 12 shillings and 21 pence!

In 1837 the Quay House and gardens were owned by John Winder Lyon Winder, Thomas Welsh was the occupier.

Henry Melling, an artist and yachtsman, lived in the house during the 1870s with his invalid niece Clara Payne. Clara could not rise from her bed, she said that *'a dame in a red cloak visited her often and that she, Clara, missed her when she departed'* who was the lady in red?
Clara died at Quay House after a slow decline in her health.

Quay House was a substantial property in its day, in 1700 it became three dwellings, and in 1803 it became a private house until 1915, now *land locked* no longer the sea lapping against its ancient walls.

By 1918 it was derelict; the Quay House finally met its fate during World War 2 when it was used for target practice. The house was finally demolished in 1944. Sadly all that remains is a few mounds of rubble with some large pieces of sandstone hidden in the undergrowth.

The Old Quay House photographed c 1930 with kind permission from Neston Library

There was a large bell which hung on the eastern gable of Quay House, it was thought to be a ships bell to warn ships entering or leaving the harbour, by 1927 the bell was no longer there.
The Quay House was reported to have had a large cellar i.e. to hold contraband; it was also reported to have had a ghost, *'a little old lady warming herself by the fire'* was this the old lady, Clara had seen? Quay House had stood for nearly 300 years, what tales it could tell, who stayed there? Where did they travel to and from? Did they ever return?

When travellers waited for the tide to turn or for the weather to subside before embarkation on their journey, they too would have sat around the open hearth, perhaps with the lady in red. Or did she frequent the alleged smugglers tunnel which was thought to have run from the Old Vicarage (now Tesco in Neston village) to the Quay House, that's a fair distance for a tunnel don't you think?

A little beyond Quay House is where the New Haven or New Quay was built at Lightfoots Pool. Due to the difficulties in vessels reaching Chester a new port was urgently needed, money was collected throughout the region to finance the project.
Work finally began on the quay in 1545 with large stones brought in from Chester; later stones were quarried from Little Neston. The King ordered 200 trees to be delivered to the Mayor for the building of the quay, funds still proved difficult over the years to complete the quay.
In 1566 the great pier of stone was overthrown in a gale, (these gales often sweep up the River Dee).

There is a document held in Cheshire Archives and Local Studies (Cheshire Shared Services) *Ref New Haven Account Book CAP/1/2*
The New Haven account lists merchants who had paid towards the building costs of the 'New Quay' between 1559 and 1598:
£6 paid for the Harbour Tallow timbers.
£3 paid for Quarrying stone in 1568.
£50 paid to John Cotton for quarrying stone.
20s 6d paid to John Burrell for carriage of timbers.
Labour cost 2d per day, Robert Crosby was paid 3d per day, was he perhaps a skilled man?
The following list records the different trades who gave money towards the cost of the 'New Haven';
3 Goldsmiths
35 Forgers and Smiths and Razor makers
6 Ironmongers
40 Glovers
51 Farmers
40 Taylors
Bankers
Butchers
Furriers
Fishmongers
Churchwardens

By aiding the survival of the 'New Haven' quay, the Merchants were endeavouring to keep shipping within the River Dee and then hence to the city of Chester. The approximate size of the quay was 56ft long 24ft wide with 11 battlements, and with embrasures for cannons! These were never used.

The quay seems in fact never to have been fully completed, due to lack of funds. The quay remained a constant burden on the City of Chester's finances. For many years Chester merchants paid taxes for the upkeep of the 'New Quay' at Neston.

Neston became a thriving port, ships not able to anchor at Chester now anchored in Neston. Liverpool at this time was still a creek with only a handful of vessels! Coaching links to London assisted in the growth of Neston. Trade imports and exports were prolific with vessels from as far as France, Spain, Ireland, and Isle of Man. Neston was prosperous, hotels were plenty, and over 1500 inhabitants lived in Neston in the 16th century.

In 1586 during the reign of Elizabeth I a hue and cry was raised; *the Spanish Armada had 700 ships headed for New Key in Worral.* It was a false report, but fear of attack from the Spanish loomed in everyone's minds. So far Wirral was safe from attack.

Importantly, even in 1282, a fleet of 60 ships anchored off Neston ready to be despatched to the Cinque Ports to help Edward I crush a Welsh uprising led by David ap Gruffydd, they then sailed to Anglesey attacked and defeated David ap Gruffydd.

In 1643 2000 soldiers left Ireland headed for New Quay, they were needed to reinforce Chester's royalist garrison during the civil war.

On 28th December 1645 the River Dee froze, causing havoc during the siege of Chester, boats supporting a bridge were sunk by floating ice. In January 1646 troops were expected from Ireland but failed to arrive due to the River Dee having frozen yet again.

In 1689 the army camped for a week at Neston waiting for fair winds to carry them to Ireland. On many occasions passengers waited weeks for fair winds to carry them to their destination.

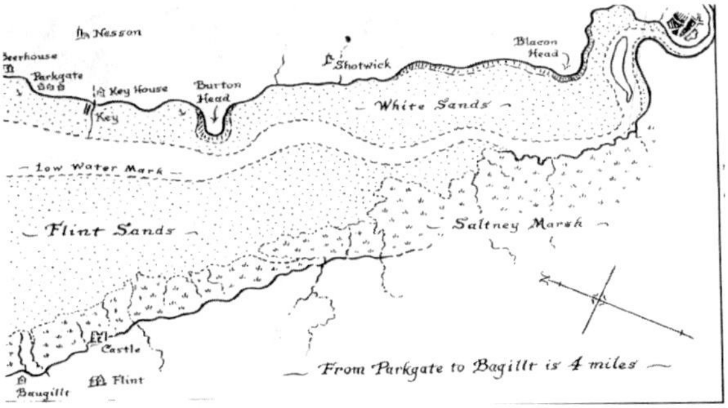

The New Quay comprised of an anchorage protected by a stone pier; in 1684 Captain Greenville Colin's chart shows the pier jutting out into the river.

Captain Greenville Collins's Chart 1684 from W Hewitt's 'Wirral Peninsula'

T A Coward wrote *at the end of the 17th century even ships of no more than 20 ton burden had to lie in a very bad harbour at Neason!.*

Silting was still causing problems all along the Wirral coast. After the New Cut was completed the channel 'Denhall gutter', which flowed along the Wirral shore, slowly prevented further use of Neston's New Quay. Finally in 1799 a new anchorage at Parkgate took over the shipping on the River Dee.

Neston was indeed a thriving town in the 1700s and 1800s. There are records of a Militia list recorded for Neston detailing a number of wives who received payment when their husbands enlisted in the Militia, see **appendix 2.**

Between the years 1809 to 1815 there are two militia lists for Chester which include many towns in Wirral, both record the men's ages and occupations, see **appendix 3.** The original documents are held in Cheshire Archives and Local Studies (Cheshire Shared Services) in Chester; the documents are a good source of local surnames ideal for the family historian.

The Wirral Peninsula provides a rich history of events on its coast, stroll along its lanes and look out over the estuary perhaps on a misty winter's day, or a warm summers evening and you will see Wirral at its best.

Now well stocked up on past events, there is a choice of two routes from the Old Quay house to Neston.

10a: Neston via Moorside Lane

Here from the 'Quay' Neston village is 2 miles distance. Across the field is a wooden footbridge which crosses the small brook whose source rises above Liverpool Road. The stream is marked on a chart in 1684 by Captain Greenville Collins. Beyond the bridge on the shoreline can be found large sandstone blocks running in a north-south direction, take a minute to look over the stones.

Keep to the path, it rises slightly then drops to a hitch hatch gate on the left. In 1834 the land here was once owned by 'Edward Mostyn Lloyd Mostyn'.
A small sandstone wall emerges into view on the right, reeds and bull rushes sway in the breeze, their winter colour a vibrant golden orange. For now the estuary is shielded from our view.

Pipe bringing water from the depths

Crossing two drainage ditches the path emerges upon a small green hillock, look down to the left, a fresh water spring gushes out of a metal pipe in the reed bed.

There are numerous springs in the locality; the water rises from subterranean sources locked in by the geological rock formations deep underground.
Five acres of land here was called Marsh or Marshfield on the Tithe maps and again was owned by the Mostyn family; it was occupied by Esther Briscoe.

Our walk continues, turn right at the hillock you will notice the old sign pointing the way back towards the 'Old Quay'.

House on Moorside circa late 1800s by kind permission from Neston Library

At the junction, cross over the road and walk past Old Quay Close, Manorial Road is on the left. Moorside Lane was once the main route to Parkgate; in 1787 the new Parkgate Road was laid.

Just a little further on your right is Old Quay Lane, turn right here past Manor Cottage. Robert Jones the headmaster rented numerous properties in the area between 1834-51 including Marsh Cottage. The Mansion on your left at the time the tithe maps were produced, was called 'Mansion Offices', again owned by the Mostyn family but occupied by John Carter. Old Quay Lane is now a quiet country lane, once it would have been a busy road winding its way to 'New Quay' or 'New Haven' as it was often called.

After a few minutes walk up the lane, large trees overhang, casting shadows across the lane. Branches meet overhead, listen you may hear the drumming of a Great Spotted Woodpecker, or perhaps catch a glimpse of it high in the trees, as I once did.

Further on up the lane you will notice a sign on a gatepost 'Old Laundry'; there was a laundry here in 1837. There was also a Well located here providing the laundry with its water, the drain for the effluent was 10 metres out into the marsh!

Just past the bend in the road a footpath sign to Neston village appears on your left, a few yards before this in the hedgerow is an old metal gate with a sign displaying: '*Neston Corporation Water Works'. No thoroughfare.*
This field was called Intake or Townfield, it's Norse for farming enclosure, there was a small coal pit recorded in this field, its location was the top right hand corner of the field.

For now walk on past the footpath on the left, carry on beyond Greenvane Nurseries Deeside Cottage (1851), and go past the entrance towards the sewer farm. On the left is a large old tree, next to the tree is a Hitch Hatch gate, go through the gate, you are now 20 metres above sea level at this point.
Walk straight ahead across the open field, cutting across your route, overgrown by trees and brambles, is the old mineral line to the colliery.

The old mineral line extension built 1876

The mineral line terminated in the area of Marshlands Road to the right, on the left it joined the West Kirby to Hooton railway line 'which is now the Wirral Way'. The mineral line extension was laid in about 1876.

Walk straight over the path of the 'mineral line' and up across the open field, the field on the left housed a pit shaft where the large pond is now. Once across the field the path crosses the Wirral Way, left goes to Parkgate, right takes you to Little Neston, for now carry straight ahead until you reach Church Lane. Turn left and walk a few yards to the wall behind the church yard of St Mary & St Helen, go through the hitch hatch gate and on up to the church.

10b: 17th century track to Neston

On reaching the 'Old Quay House' it's just a short walk of ¾ mile to Neston village.
Turn right onto the track that runs alongside the site of the old Quay House, go through the gates which cross the 17th century track then uphill to a gate at the top left of the field. Walk on the road for a few feet, there is a hitch hatch gate next to a large tree on your right, go through the gate, the stream on the right disappears into a culvert emerging on the other side of an embankment which was once part of the 'mineral line'. The routes from Moorside Lane and The Old Quay merge at this point and take the visitor towards Neston village and the church.

St Mary & St Helen Church Neston

The churches location is approximately 118ft above sea level; the first church was built by Roger de Montalt in 1170 allegedly to offset misdeeds and cruelty by his family.

Inside the church are Viking stone cross heads which were found buried in the floor and walls when the church was rebuilt in 1875. A medieval tombstone 1260 – 1280 lies there from the Order of Knights.

In 1726 Theodore Cottingham and William Young, church wardens of Neston, along with 50 parishioners petitioned the Court of Chester to prevent a gallery being built into the roof of the church, '*which would allow more light into the church'*. See **appendix 4** for a brief account of the allegation and a list of Neston parishioners who signed the petition in 1726.

There is a chapel in the church which was rescued from HMS Plymouth, one of the warships from the Falklands war, plaques commemorating the winning of two VC's can also be found in the church. On a wall inside the church you will notice a weathervane in the shape of a cockerel, the vane is dated 1747, the wood of the flagpole which was used to support it was believed to be a 100 years older! The font is octagonal and is from 1450; Neston's parish registers are quite complete and give a veiled glimpse into the social history of its parishioners.
There is much more information inside the church, have a look around it is well worth the visit.

Notes on Neston

The name Neston (*Nes-tun*) means 'farmstead at or near a promonitory' and is from Old Norse.

In 1728 King George granted a Royal charter for a weekly market and a fair three times a year. The site of the market was north of Neston Cross. In the mid 1800's many people travelled from North Wales to Neston market crossing the River Dee on foot or in carts! It must have been worth the visit, not so perhaps for markets in the 21st century. There is a record of a visitor trying to reach Neston market from North Wales and was drowned while crossing the 'sands road' over the estuary.

A court was held in Neston every fourth Monday of the month.

In the 1841 census, Neston was a prosperous town with a long list of inhabitants with worthy occupations; they included:
Shoemakers
Bakers
Tailor
Joiner
Blacksmith 'Thomas Powell'
Publicans by the dozen!
Butcher
Mason
Farmers aplenty
Miller
Surgeon
Post office 'Eliza Briscoe'
Printer
Pauper 'John Briscoe' aged 60
Miners 27
Agricultural labourers were numerous.
In the coming census of 2011 one wonders what the occupations of today's villagers would be?

The Neston Female Society was founded in 1814 to help females to help each other in times of stress and hardship, particularly after the Napoleonic war. Ladies day is the first Thursday in June and it is a great day out for everybody.

A number of references have been made to a lost road which ran along the shore at Neston.

Thomas Watkin wrote in 1886: *of a submerged Roman road at Blacon Point and off the coast at Neston.*

P Sulley in 1889 wrote; '*doubtless the Romans forged a road along the Dee, this I can think, be distinctly traced in the old road, now closed and planted over in parts, which ran through the townships of Saughall and Shotwick Park. It is very broad, almost 40 feet – was pitched in the centre, and paved, and is known to some of the oldest inhabitants as the' military road' along which troops used to march on their way to embark for Ireland. From its general character, width, and straightness, it may almost certainly be described as of Roman origin; it issued from Chester near the stone bridge over the canal, and ran through Shotwick and Neston.'*

Tantalizing thoughts of where or if, a Roman road ran along the coast at Neston or perhaps of its continuation to Meols.

Neston Village Walk

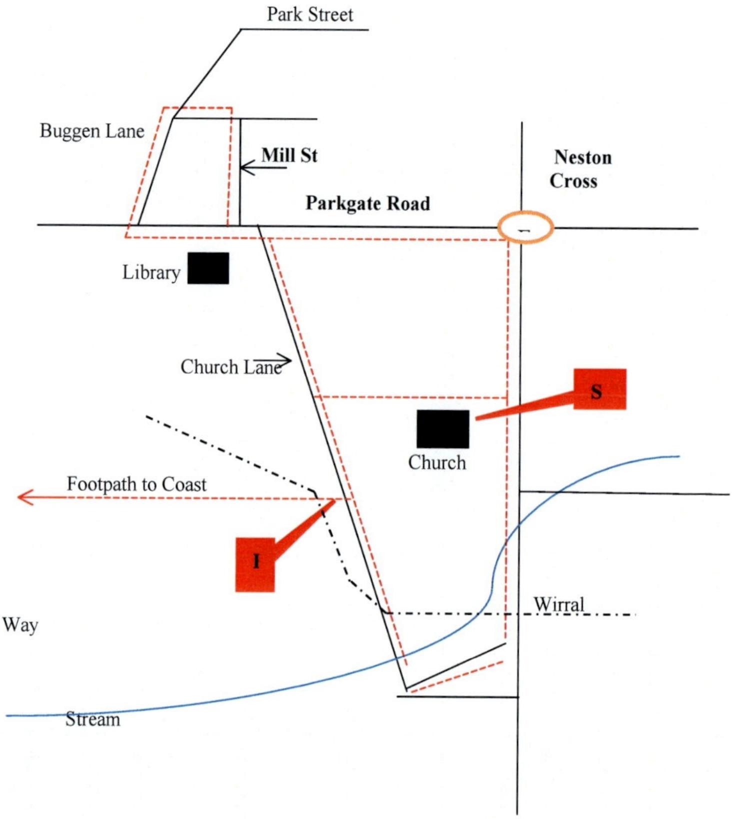

Chapter 10c: Walks around Neston village.

Leave the churchyard at the front side gate; for safety reasons, there is no footpath for a few yards directly in front of the church.

As you leave the churchyard, a footpath sign is located outside the gate together with a conservation notice and town trail plan. Walk straight on, you may notice above a shop now occupied by Martins the bookmakers is a plaque dated 1724 and the initials TM. Across the road where Tesco now stands was where the old vicarage stood in 1859, it became a girl's school, and then in 1900 it was Irwin's which was later bought by Tesco.

Neston Cross circa 1910 by kind permission from Neston Library

The fountain in the middle of the cross is Bushell's fountain. It was erected by the local community in 1882 in tribute to Christopher Bushell, a Liverpool wine merchant who installed piped water to the town.

Opposite is the Brown Horse Inn built in 1724 (one of only four pubs of that name in Britain) The oldest building in Neston is the Old Bank House here on the 'cross', built in 1703.

The White Horse Inn (demolished in 1877)
Picture by kind permission of Neston Library

On the opposite corner facing the Brown Horse Inn stood The White Horse Inn demolished in 1877. In the foreground of the picture you can see a Wheel Pump for drawing up water from the depths below. Notice the arched window in the building behind, you can still see this today!

Straight over the 'cross' and up High Street stands an ancient stone barn, perched on solid sandstone it is opposite Raby Road. A century ago much of the 'cross' was still exposed bedrock.

Now take the Parkgate Road on your left; just here is 'The Greenland Fishery Hotel' built in 1722 and was originally three houses. In 1892 the 'Black Bull' amalgamated with the Greenland Fishery Hotel with a combined licence.

W Hewitt quotes in 'Wirral Peninsula' 'that the name of the hotel derives from *'That they may have been engaged seasonally with Whaling, as vessels at Liverpool were so engaged in the 18th century'.*

Maritime records show that in 1759 HMS Vengeance arrived shorthanded in the Mersey, the press gang lay in wait, a whaling ship arrived just home from Greenland. The press gang boarded her, the crew of the whaler were ordered to board the warship but they refused. A fierce fight ensued; the whalers used long blubber knives and harpoons to drive off the press gang.

Sounds pretty terrifying, the possibility of being hauled off to no-one knows where and perhaps never to return, the crew of the whaling ship were lucky that time. Is it possible that these men fishing off Greenland gave rise to the name of the Inn in Neston?

Opposite you see a red brick tower, 'Jackson's Tower' built in 1895 by George Jackson, and he owned a chemist shop which was next door. There was a clock in the tower but it has long since gone.

A few yards on and you reach Church Lane on your left, turn here it's a pleasant walk as you pass Holly Tree house, Hermitage house and Springfield.
The imposing building on your right is 'Gascott House'; here in Church Lane was Neston's gas works. In 1832 the gas came from Birkenhead, in 1970 North Sea gas arrived in the town.

After passing Penketh House on your left, there is another hitch hatch gate and a FP sign, the path leads up to the side entrance of the church. For now walk on down Church Lane, trees overhang the lane, deep banks bound either side, to the right is the railway embankment of the Wirral Way. As Church Lane opens out a small stream passes under the road, this is the same stream which trickles its way down to the 'Old Quay'.

On your left is Eldon Terrace 1885 – 1985, walk up here to the junction with Burton Road. Then under a bridge, the 'Wirral Way' goes over the top! On your right the stream is once again allowed to flow a few yards in the open before it succumbs to its final fate as it disappears into another culvert.

Once past the mini roundabout walk straight on towards the church. Go into the Churchyard for safety reasons, (there is no footpath directly outside the church) leave again by the side gate on the right.

Turn left on to the footpath as it passes down the side of Penketh House, on reaching Church Lane turn right, and walk on till you reach the junction of Parkgate Road.

Vine House is situated across the road, to the right of the front façade of the house is a large garden wall, it is called a 'crinkle crankle' wall because it has a number of deep curves in the wall. Its purpose was to protect peaches from the frost. By lighting a fire on the opposite side of the wall from the fruit heat passed through and prevented frost damage.

Walk on to the junction of Mill Street and turn right, Hawthorne Cottage is listed on the town conservation route plan which is available at the church and the library. May Cottage with its two large garden gate pillars is sited just before you reach Townfield; a substantial large white house! Opposite Townfield is a lovely row of sandstone cottages, a little further on a large sandstone wall contains a carved wooden gate. It has long since been abandoned, owing to the large tree growing on the other side of the gate. (Gates, walls, secrets, what did I say earlier!).

Mill Street emerges at a small junction with Buggen Lane; this is a Welsh word meaning ghost! Park Street runs along to the right, one of the houses there has a date stone of 1724, and the initials TL combined with some rather pretty painted flowers.

The main entrance to Townfield is on the corner of Buggen Lane, high stone walls, a second carved gate with a fine stone portal complete the walled Townfield House, what a lovely house to live in. On reaching the end of Buggen Lane you arrive once again on Parkgate Road, turn left and head back up to Church Lane, follow this reverse route back to the 'Old Quay', or from where you started your walk.

Moorside Lane and Parkgate Parade 1 mile

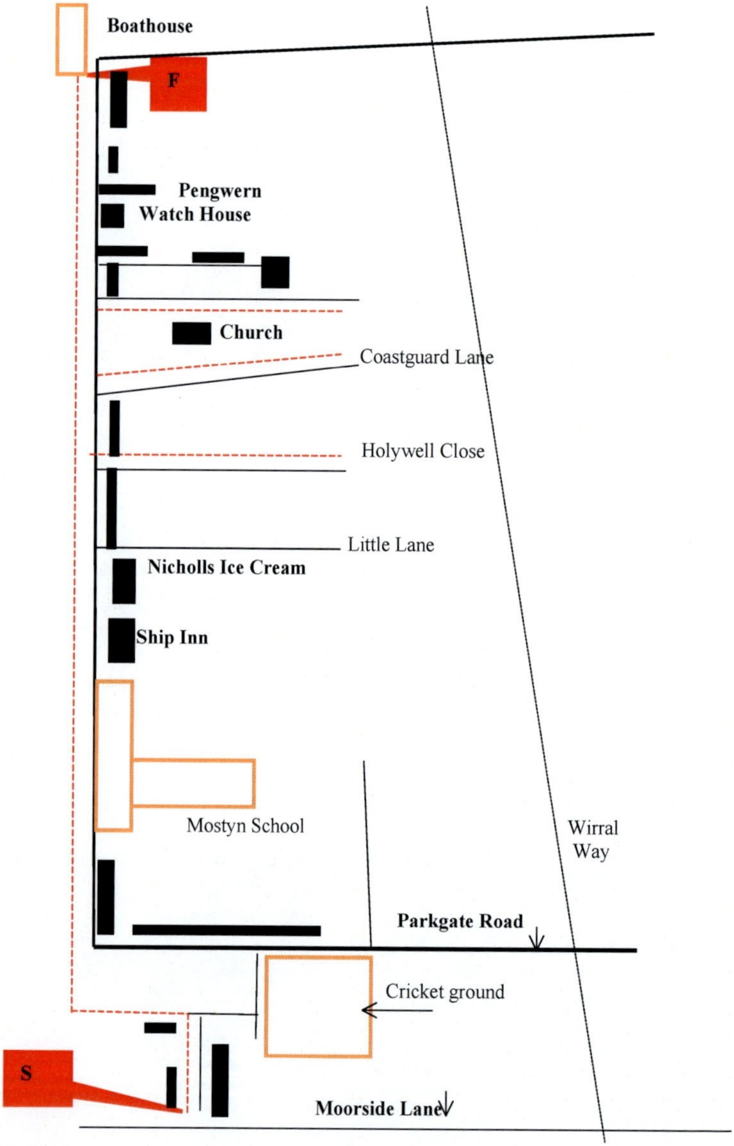

Chapter 11: Moorside Lane to Parkgate

The next part of our walk on the Wirral coast now takes us to Parkgate, a distance of ¼ mile from Moorside Lane or 1 mile from the Old Quay House. Parking can be found on Manorial Road South, it is approximately 2 metres above sea level at this point. The road was once part of the ancient highway which linked Parkgate, Moorside and Neston, now the 'highway' terminates as a cul-de-sac.

A short footpath leads on for a few yards and emerges onto a tarmac road, carry straight on until the road curves to the right.
Here on the left is Riverside House, next to the gate partially hidden by shrubs is a footpath, take this route, it continues for a few yards, then suddenly there in front of you the estuary looms large once more. The path lies next to the old sea wall, no waves today pound the wall, only tall grasses blow in the breeze. Even in 1195 a monk called Lucian from St Werburghs Abbey Chester, recorded that the sands on the River Dee where shifting.

Old quay wall in Parkgate 2010

This is a hidden stretch of wall, out of sight from the main parade which is a little further on; here these ancient blocks of sandstone up to 2 metres in length and nearly ¼ metre in depth are the cap stones for the wall.
Within a few metres the wall terminates in a large rounded sandstone block, reminiscent in shape to a metal capstan found on the docks.

Tradition states that Thomas Mostyn bought stones from the 'Old Quay' and used them for the seawalls at Parkgate.
Now the path lies on the wall itself, curving around the corner deeply rutted with the passage of time and feet! Once around the corner, the south slip on Parkgate Parade comes into view, the parade and its sandstone wall totals ¾ mile in length.

There is a total depth of 15 sandstone slabs making up the slip height, now just a few of these stones peak above the grass of the marsh, golden sands were evident here even in the 1950s, the sand now has long since vanished .

A water colour drawing by W. Herdman Parkgate in 1847.

As you reach the top of the slipway, Parkgate is set out before you, originally it was a 200 acre deer park established in 1250 by Roger de Montalt. The deer park continued for 350 years, the boundaries between Neston and Leighton were walled and gated, hence its name 'Park Gates'.
In 1801 266 people lived here , there was no mention of Parkgate in the Doomsday book only that of Leighton (Lestone) it had extensive fisheries, and it was worth *15 shillings.*

There is an old saying much written that Parkgate is being as '*all on one side*', this is typical of villages by the sea, they grow in length and retreat in land, luckily for Parkgate not much growth has occurred.

In 1717 a few houses at the waterside called 'Park Gate' were recorded, later in 1720 an anchorage was firmly established, in 1724 Parkgate had the status as a legal quay and this lasted until 1848.
Work began on the sea wall in 1800; it was never intended or used to moor ships, rather as a 'Parade' for wealthy visitors to stroll along.
From 1814 during bad weather they used 'Cheltenham Walk' it is now called the 'Rope Walk'.

On your right is the Old Quay pub built in 1963 on the site of the Old Custom House, what a shame the old building has gone, it was built in 1778 and was only demolished in the 1960s.

At the Custom House all manner of confiscated smuggled goods were sold to the highest bidder, the custom's men were also allowed to bid. Beer, wine, whiskey, silk, calf skins, soap, tea, rum, linen, handkerchiefs and wood all came under the hammer. Some goods were 'lost', and then found themselves to be in the ownership of many a customs man or local dignitary.
Smuggling was rife here in the 18th century as was the case for the rest of the Wirral Peninsula.

Across the road from the Old Quay pub is a row of cottages, the roof line shows the build over different eras:
Cottages 1- 5 were built in 1852.
Cottages 11, 14, 15, 16 where built in the 18th century.
Cottage Number 13 was built in a passage way between two houses in the early 19th century!
Others filled the gaps over the ensuing years, the oldest houses being nearer the river.

Nos. 15

Take a closer look at the ground in front of No. 15, this cottage belonged to a Chester artist named Albin Burt. In 1822 Burt was travelling between Liverpool and Chester with his nine year old son Nelson, they boarded a paddle steamer *'Prince Regent'* on the River Mersey bound for Ellesmere Port. A severe storm blew up and lasted six hours. Burt's son Nelson was swept overboard along with other passengers, they all drowned.

On his return home to Parkgate, Albin Burt set his son's name in pebbles in the earth as a reminder of his dear son, many years later the pebbles were set in cement.

No.16 was called Dover Cottage; in 1785 Emma Lyon visited Parkgate to recover from a skin complaint. Emma was reputed to have stayed at Dover Cottage, it was the last house in Station Road; she used the surname Mrs Hart during her stay to avoid unnecessary gossip. Emma was accompanied by her illegitimate daughter and her mother, Emma later became Lady Hamilton.

Parkgate Parade 2010

Now around the corner, a lovely large house 'Seaward House' has a date stone of 1721, it was a boarding school for boys from 1870 to World War One.

This house was originally the Talbot Inn (photo) 2010

The large 3 storey house right next to the road was called Green Shutters a few years ago, now the name has gone and so have the shutters! Dated as from the 1720's it was the Talbot Inn from 1764 to 1808.

Prince George, later to become King George IV, first wife, Mrs Maria Fitzherbert stayed at the Talbot Inn sometime during 1798-1799.
Mrs Fitzherbert took pity on the soldiers who were camping on the shore waiting for a boat to Ireland; she paid for extra rations for them. I'm sure they appreciated the gesture, if indeed they received the rations!

Mrs Fitzherbert married the Prince of Wales on 15th December 1785 in a secret ceremony; their marriage was void under English law due to the following facts; Prince George had not requested permission from his father or the Privy Council to marry, the marriage was held in secret, and Mrs Fitzherbert was a widowed catholic. Mrs Fitzherbert remained a mistress of Prince George until 1811.

The next house on the Parade has a striking entrance to the front door, with large stone steps and railings either side. Prospect House seems always to have been a private house, the bay windows were added in the 1860s, and fashion trends in architecture have changed a number of houses here over the years.
The large building with the black and white façade is Mostyn House, the façade dates from 1932, when the original 18c walls were in danger of collapsing.
The original part of the building was called the George Inn in 1770, in 1819 its name changed to Mostyn Arms Hotel. In 1855 Edward Price transferred his fee

paying school from Tarvin to Parkgate and the building became known as Mostyn House School.

Sir Wilfred Grenfell of Labrador was born in Parkgate in 1865; he was educated at Oxford and qualified as a Doctor, he then worked as a medical missionary with the North Sea Fishing Fleet. In 1892 he sailed a small ship across the Atlantic to Labrador in Canada in only 20 days.

Grenfell had many adventures as a young man, in 1908 at the age of 43, on his return to St Anthony in Newfoundland he was approached by two fishermen. They informed him of the plight of a young boy with blood poisoning whom Grenfell had operated on previously. Grenfell set off with his spaniel and seven huskies, he had covered 18 miles in appalling weather, the ice over which he was travelling began to break up and he was forced to take a short cut across a bay. Unfortunately for Grenfell he and his dogs became marooned on a tiny iceflow, unable to stay there long Grenfell threw lumps of ice onto a bigger iceflow, his dogs jumped in to 'fetch' the ice and pulled Grenfell into the water with them.

Grenfell's belongings went into the water and were lost, he was freezing he had to kill and skin three dogs to enable him to stay alive by wearing their pelts, giving him the warmth which was much needed. The iceflow started to drift out to open sea, but with a great stroke of luck he was seen through a telescope by the only man who owned one! The alarm was raised and he was taken to hospital, the boy Grenfell had tried to reach was also in the same hospital, both recovered. Grenfell was knighted by King George V1; Grenfell remained in Parkgate with his family, until his death in 1940 aged 75.

The Mostyn family came from North Wales; they had owned most of Great Neston and all of Parkgate since 1679. Sir Thomas Mostyn died in 1831, he never married and his estates were left to his eldest sister's husband, most of the estate was sold from 1849.

Pupils of the school in 1930 followed a sport called sand-yachting, ironically today at low tide on Hoylake beach, sand-yachting is popular, some sports don't change but the venue does!

The school had its own artesian well; it fed the water tower which was built in 1906.

Walk on past the end of the school here you will find the Ship Inn. There is a small 'weint' at the side of the Inn and the school; it was called Drury Lane, named as such to attract visitors to the area. It boasted of a theatre, a perfect

place for social gatherings, ideal for visitors and locals. In Drury Lane, apart from the farm buildings of the Mostyn Arms hotel, behind the Ship Inn, a post office, a library and a school were located.
An inn called the Bull's Head and a number of private houses were also in Drury Lane, what a busy place it must have been, in 1862 eight properties were for sale here.

Hard to separate them now when you walk up the side of the inn, only a difference in window levels, roof line and brickwork, give tell-tale signs of earlier buildings.

Why not linger awhile, take refreshments at the Ship Inn and read up on its history. The inn has had several names over the years originally it was called 'Princess Royal' named after the Parkgate Packet ship built here in 1787, last recorded in 1808. In 1820 it was the Ship Inn, then again in 1862 it was 'Princess Royal'. During this period building work took place and several properties were incorporated into the inn, it re-opened as the Union Hotel. In 1889 it was listed as a first class hotel for travellers, years later the name changed back again to the Ship Inn.

Next to The Ship is Nicholls's, famous for its ice cream, whether winter or summer everyone on the parade samples an ice cream, not tasted anything better yet, lovely!

Next on our walk is another weint 'Little Lane' an unusual collection of 18th century and 19th century cottages, No.17 Parade House was built in the early 18th century, part of a date plate is visible on the side of the house, possibly 1721. Walk up to the top of the footpath where a more interesting view of Mostyn School can be seen. Retrace your steps back to the Parade.

Parade House, South Cottage and Balcony House 2010

The next house along is South Cottage, originally its front wall was blank, no windows at all, previously there was an inn called the White Lion which stood in front of South Cottage, it was dated 1708 and was demolished in 1851. Sometime after this date bay windows were added which faced onto the river.

Within a few paces Balcony House comes into view, an obvious name don't you think? It is a late 18th century building with the balcony added during 1860-1880.

Walk up Holywell Close at the rear of Balcony House, on the upper floor is a long room called the Assembly Room; it was used for public entertainment. In 1776 a visitor noted that he paid a shilling to attend an Assembly and another shilling to play billiards. The Assembly Room was used for dancing and public gatherings, including a presentation to six fishermen who had rescued a man caught by the tide.
Its cellar was strengthened during World War Two and used as an air raid shelter.

An interesting note from World War Two, a German airman bailed out over the estuary, he was arrested and was walked ashore by Cyril Cambridge the Optician!

Carry on up the Close, large buttressed boundary walls show signs of age. Here on your left is a lovely row of sandstone cottages, six altogether tucked away from the parade, 'enchanting'. On the right is Sandheys which leads back on to Little Lane, the cottages were built in 1900. Retrace your steps back to the Parade.

Turn right, the large house set back on the right is Alma Cottage, its name taken from the Alma River in the Crimea War of 1854.
The land on which Alma Cottage is built was originally going to be used for a church; the land was sold to Henry Platt a chemist from Chester in 1855.

Across the road the seawall projects onto the marsh, an ideal place to sit and take in the view. In times past there stood a tall narrow building here built by Joseph Howard in 1730s. It was first intended as a customs house, it had a bird's eye view of the estuary! The building was also a toll house recorded in 1787. In 1812 the building was converted for public bathing, cold or warm water, or if preferred directly into the sea.
In the 1770s bathing machines were available for the more modest of visitors, by the 1840s the building had gone. With the house gone the first stretch of sea wall ended, here it was called the donkey stand. No donkeys today, but plenty of birds!

Walk on to the Red Lion, it is recorded as the oldest inn still open for business in Parkgate. In 1822 it was run by the Wood family, in 1845 it was listed as one of only two inns, the other being the Sawyer's Arms. Look up to the roof;

observe the different changes to the roof level, a number of dwellings have been converted over the years.

Carry on to Mostyn Square turn right and walk up into Coastguard Lane, the Old School house was an infants' school built in 1860, and it remained open for 107 years.

Just past the school, tucked away, are four coastguard cottages built in the 1850s, a coastguard station with a chief boatman and two or three men were maintained here until about 1875. The metal crosses in the house walls are braces to ensure the walls stability.

Walk back towards the church, it is closed at present waiting for major refurbishment turn right at the church. There is a high stone wall obscuring the view, we will find out what lies beyond later.

Mostyn Cottage was built in the 1790s it was not originally detached, the space to its left is where a public house stood in 1818. In the 1860s the cottage was a boarding school and was called Parkgate Academy.

Back onto the parade more eating establishments greet us, Marsh Cat, Mealor's fresh Shrimp, Chows, plus the pubs you have passed, have you eaten yet?

Next along our walk is another 'weint', here we find the 18th century house called Grey Walls with its heavy buttressed walls, an imposing building facing not onto the parade, but sheltering from the storms of the River Dee.
Maplewood is another 18th century building; the roof line speaks of separate building stages here.

At the top of the 'weint' is Leighton Banastre, a beautiful house set well back in the grounds, part of which we saw earlier from the confines of School Lane. The house was built by George Cripps between 1791-1795 and was originally four houses but converted to three in the 1850s.
The property called Brockleigh was a girls' school in 1810; it closed in the 1860s.

George Fredrick Handel, the composer passed through Parkgate on his return from Ireland in 1742, it has been said he stayed at Parkgate, but this has not been verified.

View of Parkgate, circa 1870's the house Grey Walls is in the background, by kind permission from Neston Library

Walk back now to the parade, the house adjoining Grey Walls is called Overdee this too is 18th century, a lovely three storey building with tiny roof lights. The picture above clearly shows in the background Grey Walls and Overdee house during the 1870-1880s

Across the road on the Promenade you will notice the metal railings again, just for a few yards; the sea wall has no parapet at this point.

In bygone days fishing nets were hung over the railings to dry and if needs be, repaired.

The cottages we now pass are Wharf Cottage and the Moorings on Mealor's Weint. Mealor is the name of a local fishing family who run the local shrimp shop of which we passed earlier.

You are now approaching the middle slip on Parkgate Parade, now only a few sandstone blocks held together with concrete tell of what was once a busy slip for the fishermen of Parkgate. Heavy stone blocks prevent access to the marsh here, but in the not too distant past fishing boats were hauled up, donkeys took sacks of cockles, mussels and shrimp by the truckload off to Parkgate station for consumers as far away as Yorkshire.

Opposite the slip is the Old Watch House which was built in 1720 by the father of John Littler. In 1799 it was leased to His Majesty's Customs as the Watch House, for obvious reasons it gave uninterrupted views of the river.

It ceased being a Watch House in 1828, when it was let to Mary Cunningham, a Bathing House Keeper!

In 1895 the local council tried to buy the property in order to widen the road at this point, but the owner asked more than the council were prepared to pay, and the road is as you find it now at its narrowest point. How fortunate for the owner, Parkgate, and its visitors, that the house remained standing.

In 1940 during the second world war a German flyer bailed out over the estuary, he knocked on the door of the Watch House and offered Francis Bushell his pistol, whereupon a cup of tea was promptly offered to the pilot.

It's amazing the history which unfolds before us as we walk along a simple tarmac road, in the Mostyn estate papers of 1732 it records Parkgate with no road fronting the beach.

Up on the rise sits White Cottage, it is thought an ancient cottage called 'Chapel Cottage' was incorporated into the present building; it was originally the home of an actor called Samuel Ryley (c1758-1837).

Walk on down to the two properties surrounded by a large sandstone wall, Brooke House (1904) and Westbrook. The land they occupy was recorded in the Tithe maps as Dock Fields owned by Rt. Hon. E Mostyn and occupied by Elizabeth Ellis.

No longer the Dock Fields, but two properties stand before you; Brooke House was owned and designed by the architect W Aubrey Thomas who also designed the Liver building! It is quoted that the owner raised the wall of the garden so that his three beautiful daughters could sit outside without being ogled by passers-by. Sounds as though it's from a fairy tale!

We have nearly finished our walk along Parkgate Parade, mostly looking inland at the houses, now and again stopping to look westward over to Wales.
No matter what time of day or night there is always something to draw your eye and your thoughts here on the edge of the river, it's a peaceful area with plenty of resting places along the way.

Have you spotted Flint Castle, Point of Ayr, or Mostyn docks, on a clear day they are easy to spot on the opposite side of the river in North Wales.

When the mist comes in the Welsh coastline is shrouded from our view completely, sometimes twinkling lights can be seen in the distance peeping through the mist, the only reminder that there is a coast there at all. It reminds me of the film 'The Fog' scary stuff!

Next along is 'Pengwern' a lovely three storey house built early 18th century, or possibly earlier, as an Oak staircase is thought to be 17th century. Adjoining these along a little 'weint' are four cottages; Pendle Cottage, Reeds Cottage,

Dee Cottage and Sawyer's Cottage, all 18th century; they were not recorded on a map dated 1732. In 1828 they were known collectively as 'Pengwern'.

In 1793 Sawyer's cottage was called 'Sawyers Arms', it was an alehouse and its original landlord was named Richard Bartly, he also had another occupation that of a carpenter, many landlords indeed many people had various skills to enable them to survive. In 1960 during alterations to Sawyer's cottage, a coin dated '1694' was found in a wall.
The alehouse had a cellar, it was built in the form of a brick vault, but it was above the ground due to the soil being too damp for conventional cellars.
It has also been said that a passage ran from the back of the alehouse up the rise beyond, it was filled in when it became unsafe. Perhaps it was used for a hasty retreat removing contraband away from the eagle eyes of the customs men!
Now when you look at the pretty cottage it is not difficult to imagine its past activities all those years ago. The sea lapping just a few feet away, boats hauled onto the beach, nets drying in the sun, smugglers trying to move their contraband to safer hideouts!

In 1802 it was recorded; *an old woman was drowned in her bed at Dee Cottage when a heavy storm flooded the area.*

The Boathouse Inn is just a few yards away, there is a small slipway mostly overgrown, hardly noticeable now, but picture the scene: a heavy sea, gale force winds, dark menacing clouds ready to let fall its load, tiny boats being tossed about the sea trying to make to the safety of the land. Disaster strikes, ships founder, their cargoes crew and passengers thrown into the sea, later the cargo washes up on shore ready to be spirited away. Some people survive the ordeal others sadly do not.

There have been many shipwrecks on the River Dee and its estuary.
The following list gives evidence of just a few of the tragedies that befell shipping on the River Dee;
1642 *A ship belonging to Mr Johnson sprang a leak, the ship filled with water, her cargo spoilt.*
1708 *Severe storms 22 boats wrecked.*
1758 *A ship bound for Dublin was lost 70 died, 19 people were arrested for interfering with the bodies found on the beach.*
1779 *Two women drowned when the ferry overturned; it was moored behind the Boathouse or 'Beerhouse'* as it was then known.
1775 *Two boats lost in a storm on the Dee.*
1775 *The Parkgate packet 'Nonpariel' was lost on Hoyle bank her master was Samuel Davis, the wind raged for 30 hours many passengers and cargo were*

lost. Its cargo of silk, spices, and jewels were valued at £20,000 even then! Many bodies were found washed up on Talacre and Gronant beach.
1796 *The ship the 'Queen' was wrecked.*
1806 *Between September and October storms raged along the coast the 'King George' sank with only four sailors and one boy spared, 120 drowned.*
1882 *William Smith aged 15 was carried off course, he died from exposure.*
1920 *A fisherman named Mellor was drowned.*
1922 *Another fisherman named Mellor was drowned.*
Many more have lost their lives, or their livelihood, over the years exposed here on the River Dee and its estuary.

In 1866 *William Duncan, William Dungill, William Lang and William Woods had paid to Chester Court a fee for holding Salmon Stake nets in the River Dee;* the fishing industry was still active though on a much smaller scale. Travellers and locals past and present could tell a fine tale of fear, enlightenment, hope, sadness or perhaps enjoyment here on the River Dee!

Parkgate to Thurstaston 3¾ up to 7 miles

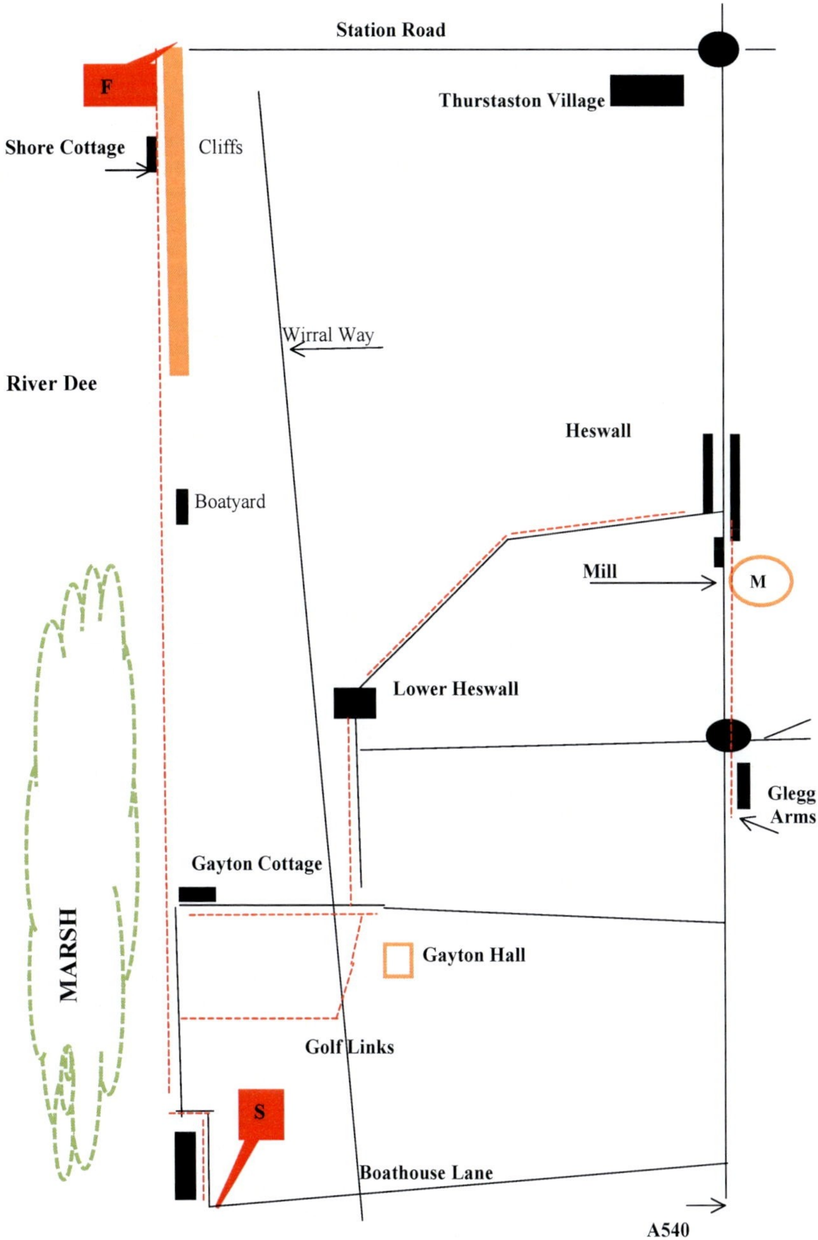

Chapter 12: Parkgate to Thurstaston

This is a walk of 3¾ miles along the coast from the Boathouse at the end of Parkgate Parade to Shore Cottage on Thurstaston beach. There are also additional walks to Lower Heswall of 1¼ mile, or to Gayton Hall via the golf links and Gayton Cottage from the Boathouse ,a walk of 2¾ mile. Whichever route you choose there are interesting snippets of history along the way.

Walk past the Boathouse down the tarmac road with the marsh on your left. An open grassy area comes into view, this was the site of Parkgate Baths the area on the old maps was called 'Slang' by the shore, (it means narrow strip of land).

As you walk beyond the 'baths' you reach a large sandstone wall, on the left there is a flight of steps embedded in the wall. Walk up the steps, mind the nettles, or go through the gate on your right, a vista opens up before you, an open sky with a fine view to Hilbre and Point of Ayr in North Wales.

At the time of writing the sky is dark with heavy clouds over towards Flint, but out towards Anglesey the weather is still clear.
Once you have climbed the steps you are now on top of the sea wall, its large worn sandstone blocks protrude above the marsh by a height of 2 metres.
It's a lovely walk here even in bad weather, opposite the steps in the wall there is a route to the Wirral Way if an alternative route is preferred. The sea wall curves to the right, the route is along the sea wall, its stone worn with the passage of time and feet. The wall at its base is showing four courses of sandstone, the rest are far below the level of the marsh. The grass is high and very dense; dozens of butterflies dance from stem to stem, while Herons, Gulls, and Curlews call in the distance.

A few yards out into the marsh is a large tract of water, it's what's left of the main channel for Parkgate, the 'Beerhole' relates to a deep anchorage which was recorded on a number of old maps.

Walking along the seawall, green fields open up on the right; Backwood Hall is in the distance. Within a few minutes the path crosses a wooden bridge over a ditch draining the fields on the right. Look into the ditch through the vegetation, the sea wall curves around the ditch to the right with some intricate brick work, quite fancy for a ditch! Perhaps when the wall was built the curve created a mooring on the leeward side of the wall offering some protection from the wind!

A few yards on from the 'ditch' there is a slip way largely overgrown, sandstone blocks are laid on the floor forming the slip itself with two upright sandstone pillars looking out over the estuary. Here in the past, cattle swam to shore from the main channel after being unloaded from ships anchored there. There was a house and a croft here in 1837 and was occupied by James Duncan. The walk carries on; the wall curves again to the right, the sandstone blocks are larger in size here, and approximately 2 metres above the marsh.

The track adjacent to the wall is littered with small pieces of sandstone and concrete, over to the right is Heswall Golf Course founded in 1902.
The drainage ditch we crossed a few yards back was the ancient boundary of Leighton and Gayton.

On a clear bright day you can see for miles, the hill on the right is Poll Hill at 365ft the highest point on the west coast of Wirral. Here on the marsh a few feet below the path, large pieces of timber have been washed up by a high spring tide; they lay bleached by the sun.

Away across the marsh Flint castle catches the sun's rays, the castle was built by King Edward I in 1277. Turn your gaze back towards Parkgate, its position on a bend in the coastline gives fine views along the coast, ideal for navigation.

Now yet another drainage ditch water is piped under the path from the golf course and drains onto the marsh, a small pool is formed by the water as it tumbles out of the pipe, tiny fish dart about the fresh water pool, no doubt trying to escape the eagle eye of predators!

There is a choice of two routes to Gayton Cottage:

The first route of 2¾ miles to Gayton Cottage past Gayton Hall, take the footpath over the golf links, where two paths cross take the left turn, this is the ancient track to Gayton Hall, it's a private residence hidden away from view amidst woodland. In 1330 Gayton Manor passed in marriage to Gilbert Glegg, it remained in their care until 1758 when William Glegg died without issue. The manor passed to his niece Mary, wife of John Baskervyle, the name Glegg was then added to his surname.

Gayton Hall was built in 1663, partly brick with a wood frame interior, the hall was once protected by a moat, it also had a columbarium (dovecot). Gayton Hall was mentioned in the Hearth taxes between the years 1663 – 1688, eight chimneys were recorded for the hall.

In 1689 William of Orange stayed at the hall while on his way to Hoylake en route to Ireland, in return for Gleggs hospitality he conferred a knighthood on Glegg. In honour of this Glegg planted two fir trees named William and Mary, one of the trees fell during a storm in 1936 the other a little while later.

In 1835 the Tithe maps record the hall belonged to another John Baskervyle Glegg; it was occupied at the time by William Latham. The Gleggs owned the hall until 1921.

Continue up the lane its steep banks show its antiquity as it twists its way up the hill. Just around the bend the entrance to the hall is observed, continue on until you reach Gayton Farm Lane. Here is the old coach house belonging at one time to the hall, a few yards on turn left onto Cottage Lane then walk down towards Gayton Cottage.

The second route to Gayton Cottage is along the shoreline, stay on top of the wall, reeds sway and rattle in the breeze, the only sound except for the birds. Don't be tempted to walk over the marsh, there is no path and it can be extremely dangerous.

Gayton Slip and harbour wall 2010

Suddenly around a bend the wall abruptly terminates with a flight of three steps which take you to marsh level and Cottage Lane. Here lies Gayton Cottage complete with harbour wall.

Gayton or '*Gaitone' as it was recorded in the Doomsday book in 1086 was held by Robert of Rhuddlan, it had:*
1 hide paying geld, it had land for 2 ploughs.
2 villeins and 3 bordars with 1 plough worked the land.
It also boasted of 2 fisheries it was worth 15 shillings then 3 shillings after the conquest.

The 'fishing' would have been from the anchorage at this point on the River Dee. The name Gayton is derived from; *Geit* meaning goat, and *tun* for enclosure or farmstead; it's one of a number of places where combined elements of Norse and Anglo Saxon have been used.

Gayton Cottage was a former ferry house and stage coach stop, its location at the side of a creek was a key element in its history. The present building was recorded on Greenwood's map of 1819, while as long ago as 1277 King Edward I was believed to have crossed to Flint from here.

The Chester High road at the junction of Gayton Lane was the main Turnpike Road, there were partial remains of a toll cottage opposite Gayton Lane where the stables are now, it was believed to be last occupied in 1965; in 1981 a windowless single storey building existed.

To visit Heswall Old Village, it's approximately ¾ mile away, walk up Cottage Lane, turn left at the T junction onto Gayton Road walk straight on towards Heswall old village.

Heswall's church of St Peters is a little further, built on a slight rise it gives lovely views from the rear of the churchyard. It's a pleasant place to visit at any time In September 1875 during a severe storm, lightning struck the church; the organist was killed, as too was the bellows boy.

Heswall was mentioned in the doomsday book, it was recorded as Essulwall home of Essul possibly a Norse settlement in the 8th or 9th century.

To walk to Heswall shops and eating establishments, proceed up School Lane which is next to Black Horse Inn, then onto Rocky Lane, emerging onto Telegraph Road near the bus station. A ten minute walk on Telegraph Road will take you to Gayton Mill, it's now a private house, the mill was built 1733-1735 it worked until the 1870s. One mill owner's wife bore him 16 children; it must have been pretty cramped! In 1904 it was derelict; planning permission was sought in 1990 for the mill and a small estate.

Beyond Gayton Mill is the Glegg Arms, it's a nice place to eat. In 1840 it was called Crabb's Inn after the landlord Edward Crabbe, and in 1892 J Brownlie was the publican, it then became known as the Glegg Arms. There used to be a weighbridge in the front of the single storey building, in 1904 a veranda was built to shelter penny slot machines!

Retrace your route to Gayton Cottage.

There is a choice of two routes to Thurstaston, the first is along the Wirral Way, this route can be reached by walking up Cottage Lane; take the path on the left which leads down onto the Wirral Way then turn left, this will take you to Thurstaston.

The second route is along the marsh, good stout waterproof boots or shoes are advised, the path can be pretty boggy. Walk on the marsh past Gayton Cottage; it may be useful to use insect repellent, midges and mosquitoes can be troublesome during the summer months. It's a ten minute walk to Riversbank Road and is a very quiet stretch, just birds bees, and butterflies.

It can be a little wet at first; the reeds tall and stately are swaying in the breeze, a well-trod path meanders through the reeds, the sandstone sea wall which bounded Gayton Cottage continues northwards along the coast.

The reeds now reaching a height of over 3 metres, the grassy path is still quite clear although you do need to push the reeds out of the way sometimes. A few yards out on the marsh is Heswall Gutter sometimes known as 'Gayton 'Gutter, it's quite deep during high tide, the Gutter runs parallel with the coast from here. Beyond the Gutter; Hawks hover over their prey, a Heron treads daintily over the reeds towards a small clearing then nestles down to rest. The sandstone wall continues to keep us company along the marsh, sometimes it's lost beneath brambles, gorse or reeds, only to emerge a little later on. At the bottom of Riverbank Road, a footpath leads up to a very large embankment 6-7 metres in height with a car park at the top, part of the sandstone is encased with concrete, quite ugly but necessary.

Continue on the marsh, it's a little wet underfoot to begin with, but then after a few minutes a good grassy path leads us on. The sea wall still retains its height, a steep slipway runs down the side of the embankment allowing access to the marsh. Partially hidden by reeds a large rubber buoy lies deflated in the reeds, no doubt washed up by a high spring tide. The path is clear ahead, the sandstone wall now clearly in view once again, like a dear friend!
Onward past another flight of stone steps flanked with painted blue railings, more houses come into view, another footpath leads onto Seabank Road, the sandstone wall has disappeared here, perhaps robbed out over the years.

The marsh path heads north through another reed bed, the land on the right is elevated to about 5 metres, here only grass and clay, no sandstone.

The Gutter still runs parallel with the coast, and the sandstone wall is back only for a few yards as we approach Marine Drive, once again concrete encases the wall, a flight of steps lead up to the road.

Continue on the marsh, a drainage ditch trickles out at the base of the wall; at this point sandstone blocks cover the concrete, aesthetic perhaps? Here on the grass you will notice thousands of tiny crab shells washed up by high tide and bleached by the sun. Beyond, the Gutter holds onto its flotilla of little boats during low water when only the tops of the masts can be seen. Some boats lie in channels off the main Gutter; again only the top of the masts could be seen, it reminded me of the film 'African Queen' with Humphrey Bogart.

The mud flats either side of the Gutter are cracked and baked in the heat of the sun, bird's footprints by the hundred are found embedded in the mud waiting for the next tide to cover them. The grass and reeds are interspersed with flowers; the bees are drawn to their nectar, it has been a poor year for honey bees this year (2009), a virus has greatly reduced their numbers.

The sandstone wall which has kept us company for the last mile or so has now gone, replaced by a low cliff protecting the hinterland from the sea. Rowan trees, Blackthorn, Briar and Dog Rose cover the cliff, excellent views of Parkgate can be observed from here.
As you look back the coast curves gently out towards Wales, past Parkgate the hillock in the distance topped with trees is Burton Point where the Iron Age Fort is, it has a great advantage as a look-out post doesn't it? The view of the river is breath taking as you look out across the estuary to North Wales and beyond.

A few more yards and we arrive at Banks Road; the restaurant Sheldrake's is bustling with customers, although none are sitting outside today.

Heswall 'Gayton' Gutter from Heswall Boatyard 2009

Formerly the Dee Sailing Club was located here before the silting became too severe for the sailing boats to operate. A boatyard now stands in its stead; boats large and small are crammed into the tiny yard, masts tall and lofty blow in the breeze their lines clanking loudly, as if wanting to be back on the open sea. Large iron capstans sit either side of a small gulley, boats rest on trailers waiting to be hauled into the boatyard, while others are waiting to put back to sea.

An old man sitting by the capstan mends his nets; this little snapshot in time would have been mirrored up and down the river many years ago.

In Banks Road are a number of tiny cottages, these belonged to Heswall fishermen, two families were prominent in the late 1860s; the Brierly and Evans families. In the 1901 census three families with the name Brierly still lived in Banks Road Cottages.

Continuing the walk to Thurstaston; the sun shone for me this particular late summer morning, the tide was out, huge drifts of Sea Asters [*Aster tripolium*] a native plant of the salt marshes flourishes here. The blue flowers with yellow centres sit above fleshy leaves, their perfume on a warm day is quite intoxicating, bees and butterflies find them irresistible.

The path at this point can be muddy after rain but only for a few yards, the sandstone wall which has been our companion for some time has not returned, in its place an embankment of grass and gorse.

Old boats lie damaged and abandoned high on the mud flats, some well above high water level. The Gutter is deep and wide at this point and is today's anchorage for both fishing and leisure boats. The path along the shore follows a new sea defence; concrete and steel protect the sewage farm above. Beyond, large boulders have been placed along the coast to assist the new sea defence, drainage outlets issue on to the marsh from the headland, which is starting to rise quite quickly.

The high water mark is prominent here; seaweed has been piled up onto the beach along with old dinghies, and sadly large quantities of plastic bottles. Mud flats now replace the grass covered marsh; a stream babbles over the sand into the river, the stream started its life above 'The Dungeon' where it cuts deep into the sandstone bedrock then crosses the headland, now it trickles into the River Dee.

Across the field is Broad Lane formerly named Warmby Lane, this is the place of an ancient Norse settlement named Warmby 'Varmr-byr' meaning Warm settlement. It is one of many 'lost' settlements only to be found now in field or road names. Target Road is off Broad Lane; in World War One the artillery practised firing their guns out over the river from Target Road.

Within a few yards the cliffs now begin to rise quite steeply, 5-7 metres at first; on the headland above, wooden seats have been placed for visitors to rest awhile and admire the scenery. The path now is over a bed of gravel, possibly left from where the boulder clay has been washed out from the cliffs over many hundreds of years. The cliffs show evidence of recent land falls, don't be tempted to climb them they are unstable and therefore dangerous.

One such land fall leaves a large mass of boulder clay four to five feet high resting on the sand, its once hidden contents of pebbles now exposed, seeing the sun for the first time since they were consumed by the ice flows that carried them down from the north of Britain.
Flint, Granite, Shale, Quartz, Slate, Marble and Limestone to name but a few, had been carried along with mud and ice from as far away as Scotland and the Lake District. Now they lie on the beach, released from their mud tomb for us to marvel at 10,000 years after being consumed.

Boulder clay cliffs on Thurstaston beach 2009

Stretches of cliff now reach a height of over 12 metres, a sheer face of solid boulder clay, its base studded with bands of shale; the cliff is slowing being undercut by high spring tides.
Parts of the cliff are being eroded from behind; rivulets of rain water run off the cliff and cut deep into the boulder clay, eventually separating them from the headland. Somewhat like miniature sea stacks!

The Wirral Country Park is above us, there is no access yet. Walk along the beach for a while, the cliffs are a deep red colour here. Another small stream issues onto the beach from a deep ravine in the cliff, this stream starts its life below Thurstaston Hall.

Wooden steps lead up towards Thurstaston visitor centre, why not spend time on the beach, the cliffs here are over 20 metres high.

In 1875 this area is recorded as Dawpool its name meaning 'small port'.
The Tithe map of 1831 records the name of the cliff as 'The Banks ',the land owner was Joseph Morgan. Where the ravine cuts into the cliff the field was named 'Part Dawpool Meadow', beyond that 'Dawpool Meadow', these were the only two fields to have the name of Dawpool.

Shore Cottage on Thurstaston Beach 2009

Beyond the stream is Shore Cottage occupied once by Sally McCrae, who died in 1953. The cottage was recorded on a map of 1875.
It was previously a coastguard station believed to be built on the sight of the Customs House which closed in 1793 due to lack of shipping.

'Speeds' map of 1611 does not record Dawpool; in 1689 Captain Greenville records Dawpool as a deep anchorage, there is no quay at Dawpool, what may be all that remains of one is a long line of sandstone blocks running north to south with many broken smaller stones lying inward of the larger blocks.

In 1769 it was recorded that a William Parkinson was stationed at Dawpool, he was a Customs Riding Officer. In 1820 a steamboat project was drawn up for Dawpool, a survey was completed but the project was abandoned. Omerod and Mortimer both mentioned that a ruin of an Old Hall or Castle stood at the edge of the river at this point. Nothing remains of such antiquity now, having long since crumbled into the river or its stone robbed away!

The beach is slightly raised here, deep scars split the cliffs, the cottage hugs the base of the cliff both of which are exposed to high spring tides and gales which frequently blow up the River Dee.

The Dungeon, Oldfield and Thurstaston Common a walk of up to 3 ½ miles

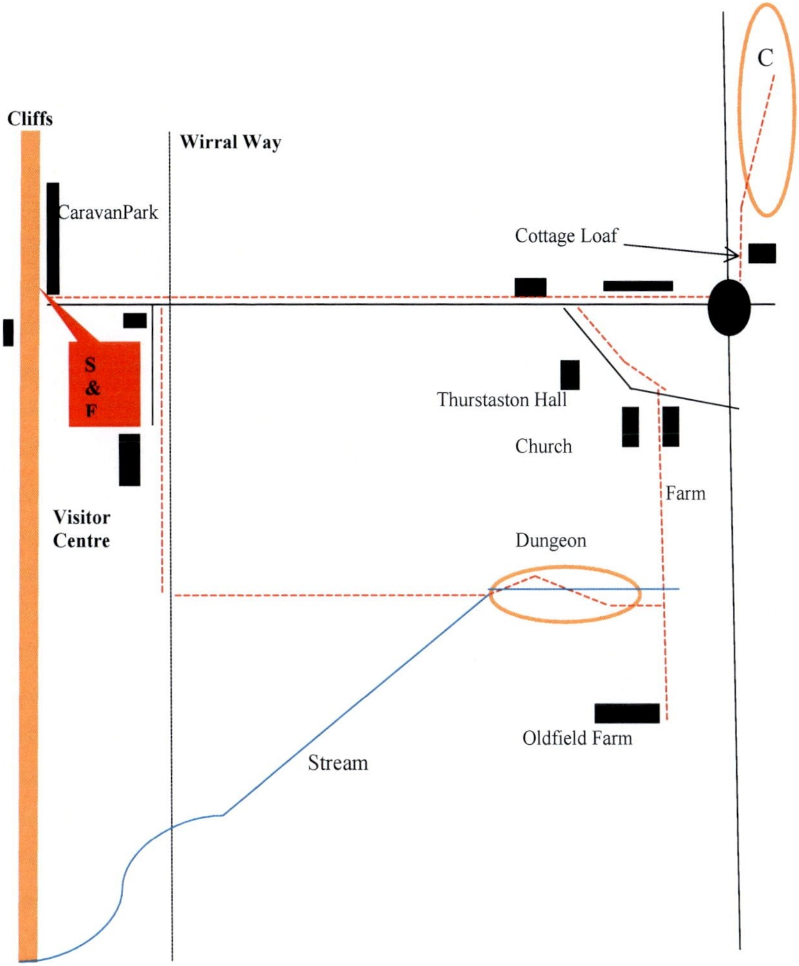

Chapter 13: To the 'Dungeon'

Now for the next part of the walk, inland to Thurstaston visitor centre and then on to the 'Dungeon', follow the steps up from Shore Cottage and turn right to cross the fields towards the visitor centre. Take care on the cliff edge they can be dangerous places. During World War Two there were gun emplacements here on the headland; the concrete footings are hidden under the turf. Many a time I have walked this way with my children and my grandchildren, the visitor centre being a good place to stop and read up on the history of the area.

The location of Thurstaston's railway cutting, if you have not already noticed, is quite a distance from the village or other habitation. This in part was due to Thomas Ismay who built Dawpool house in Thurstaston and did not wish to have the railway too close to his home. As chairman of the railways at the time, he had some say in its location!

The disused railway line was opened as the Wirral Country Park in 1973; it was the first country park in Britain. The Wirral Way starts at West Kirby and finishes at Hadlow Road Hooton, it's a great walk and fairly flat all the way, the route provides access for horses and can be used by cyclists too.

Thurstaston station still has its elevated platform levels, but Hooton station is complete with ticket office and looks as though the station master has just popped out!

Path to the Dungeon 2007

To access the Wirral Way at Thurstaston leave the visitor centre, turn right and walk along the Wirral Way for a few hundred yards. There is a sign which points the way to the 'Dungeon', turn left here and follow the path.

On your left a stream etches deep into the sandstone bedrock, climb on up the hill, the tree cover is quite dense here; this area was called 'Fox Cover' in the tithe map of 1831. The land was owned by John Baskervyle Glegg.
The stream has magnificently eroded the soft Bunter sandstone, creating a deep ravine. There are plenty of places to stop, rest and play. Children find hollows to

hide in pretending to be smugglers hiding their loot! Lots of places to scramble over, but caution must be observed.

The 'Dungeon' and my family 2007

Whatever the weather, snow, sun or rain it's a delight to venture into this magical place. As you stand in the large hollow with cliffs all around, take the path on the left of the ravine. When you reach the top of the cliff keep right and stay on the path, don't stray too near the edge!

The stream which tumbles down the cliff can be just a trickle, in winter it looks lovely when the water has turned to ice; this is the only waterfall in Wirral.

A view down the ravine into the Dungeon 2009

The walk on the rise here is very gentle, look down into the ravine; it's a good drop down to the bottom. The tiny stream has been gouging its way deeper and deeper over many thousands of years!

Moss covered sandstone lies in the river bed, a small cliff of silt stone is showing on the south side of the ravine, this is due to faulting of the older Wilmslow sandstone.

Duck boards, stone flags and a stony path now lead the way up through the woods, the stream drops from 250ft to 100ft in a third of a mile. In 1987 the area was designated a Site of Special Scientific Interest due to its interesting geology exposure. The area is covered with Oak, Elm, Beech, Sycamore, Alder, scrub and heath.

The path leads on up a slight rise, a number of drainage ditches have been cut across the path to aid the drainage of fields on the right, within a few yards you reach a signpost, turn right for Heswall, left for Thurstaston. Before we leave this area you may find 'Oldfield' an interesting place to visit, if so turn right towards Heswall.

To Oldfield

The return trip to Oldfield is ¾ mile, the path is slightly up hill then along a good path until you reach the corner of four fields, here is a gigantic sandstone pillar, at one time a gate post, but why is it so big?
Go through the next gate and walk uphill, the views here are outstanding; the estuary and the Welsh hills offer the walker a chance to stop, rest and gaze, lovely.

The ground drops away quite suddenly here towards the coast, in the distance the hedgerow nearest to the coast is the course of the stream from the 'Dungeon' searching for its final destination before spilling out over the sand.
It lies very close to the 'lost' settlement of Warmby; perhaps the early Norse settlers used the fresh stream water as their water supply!

The path turns right here, go over an old stone stile, the farm yard is just around the bend, the rear of Oldfield Farm comes into view an array of different building styles. The main part of the farmhouse can be viewed from the front, just a peek through the hedgerow mind! The building in 1831 showed a number of wings to the property, it was owned by William Lloyd and occupied by John Baskervyle Glegg, here's that fellow again.
The house was built by Sir Rowland Stanley of Hooton in 1604, there is a date stone with his initials; *'RS 1604'*. Sir Stanley died here in 1614 aged 96; sadly he only lived there for 10 years but what a lovely place to end your days.

Oldfield was given to Guy de Provence on his marriage to Alice sister of Sir Patrick Haselwalle, he was sheriff here in 1288, and a grandson Richard assumed the name of Oldfield.

The Manor of Oldfield was not recorded in the Doomsday book it was most likely to have been under the manor of Heswall 'Eswelle'

It's such a quiet spot hidden away from the urban spills of Heswall. It has been recorded in a book, 'Spooky Liverpool', that Oldfield Farm was haunted.
Billy Roberts, upon staying at the farm, witnessed luminous mists in the bedroom, also whispers and strange noises occurred.

On windy nights the wind would whistle through the stone walls, ghostly lights and dark shapes were witnessed in the courtyard, figures were seen making their way toward the estuary! Spooky indeed, who were they, has anyone else seen them?

Now retrace your steps back to the sign post pointing the way to Thurstaston just above the 'Dungeon'. Onwards to Thurstaston church a short distance of ¾ mile, opposite the signpost a stream trickles down the hill from the field beyond and on towards the coast.
Go through the gate, you can hear the traffic now from the A540; blot it out, look at the hedgerows instead. Here grow wild roses, hawthorne and brambles, at the time of writing in September there is an abundant supply of rosehips and blackberries all waiting to be picked.

The large hollow on the left is recorded as a pond on the Tithe map of 1838, through another gate up a slight incline then its downhill all the way, and right in your line of sight is the tower of St Bartholomew's church. A few more gates then the path leads onto a farm road, the farms on the right and left in 1837 were owned by John Baskervyle Glegg, as too was Thurstaston Hall. Church Farm on the right makes for a pleasant day out, especially if you have young children.

Chapter 14: Thurstaston Church and Common

Walk around to the front of the church and enter through the main gate. Cast your eyes upon the war memorials from both world wars, so many people lost their lives, all are commemorated here who came from the local community. One such man was Frank Lester VC, he was in the 10th Battalion Lancashire Fusiliers, and his Victoria Cross was sold at auction for £78,000 and was purchased by the Michael Ashcroft Trust.

Frank Lester aged 22 was killed 12th October 1918 in Neuvilly France; he was killed by a German sniper.
"He observed that an enemy sniper was causing heavy casualties to a party in a house across the street. Pte Lester exclaimed 'I'll settle him' and dashing into the street shot the sniper at close quarters, falling mortally wounded at the same instant. Frank Lester knew it was certain death to go into the street and the party opposite faced with the alternative of crossing the fire-swept street, on staying they would have been shot one by one. To save their lives Lester sacrificed his own"
He is buried in Neuvilly communal cemetery three miles north of Le Catecu row B Grave 15. Lester's name is also on the family grave in Holy Trinity Hoylake, his parents were John and Ellen Lester 'Market Gardener's from Miller's Hay in Irby.
What a sad but heroic story.

The church is the third church to be built on this site, in 1724 the church was within the courtyard of Thurstaston Hall, in 1724 the church was described as a mean building; there is a picture of it in the British museum.

In 1820 the church was demolished and the second church was built, it was a plain stone building; the tower from this church still stands in the graveyard behind the church.

Thurstaston's Old Church Tower 2009 and a view of Thurstaston Hall

In 1871 a meeting was held and an agreement was reached on pulling down the second church, and approval was given for the erection of a third church.

Joseph Hegan of Dawpool's executors set aside £4500 for the new church, built of local sandstone inside and out, the new church was completed in 1886. The church was erected in honour of Joseph Hegan by his daughters, Joseph Hegan also built Dawpool School in 1858, and later a new school was built nearer Thurstaston common. The walls of the churchyard are built from the stones of the second church!

Thurstaston or *'Turstanetone'* was recorded in the Doomsday Book of 1086 *it was held by Robert de Rhuddlan he was given the land by Hugh Lupus first Earl of Chester. Prior to this in 1086 it was held by Leofnoth he was a free man.*
Thurstaston had 2 hides paying geld land enough for 4 ploughs
In demesne there was 1 plough and 2 Oxmen.
4 villeins 4 bordars with 1½ ploughs shared.
It was worth 30 shillings before TRE, after it was worth 8 shillings, now it was worth 16 shillings.'

The land was becoming valuable again!

Robert de Rhuddlan held Thurstaston, Caldy, Meols and Wallasey without beholding to another Lord, the remainder of the land he owned in Wirral he held with other Lords or to William King of England.

Robert de Rhuddlan was cousin to Hugh of Chester, Robert held nine villages in Wirral together with their land, and he was Wirral's largest landowner.The second largest landowner was the Church, third was William Malbank, then finally the Earl of Chester who held only three villages within Wirral at the time of the Doomsday Book. After the death of Robert de Rhuddlan the land passed to the Montalt family, Lords of Mold and Hawarden, it then passed to the Haselwalls.

Why not wander around the graveyard; you will notice a large tombstone to Thomas Ismay and his wife.

Dawpool *1884 R. Norman Shaw, architect.*
From the book written by A.H. Gardner 'Outline of English Architecture'

Thomas Ismay built 'Dawpool', he pulled down the previous house built by Joseph Hegan in 1865. Ismay completed the new 'Dawpool' in 1884 the year of his silver wedding. Ismay was the founder of the White Star Line he was a wealthy and important man of his time.

The main Heswall to West Kirby road ran too close to Ismay's home, so he paid for a new cut to be made through the sandstone of Thurstaston hill, this relocated the road further from his eyes and ears! Understandably geologists see the exposed strata as a 'walk through time'.

Sadly 'Dawpool' was demolished in 1927 and the land sold as building plots, Ismay also had cottages demolished, and closed the village pubs. Thomas Ismay very much changed the village of Thurstaston perhaps that is why it has survived as a tiny microcosm with just the Hall and Church as the vocal point! Thomas Ismay's son Bruce was one of the survivors of the ill-fated liner 'Titanic'.

When you leave the church take a look at the large gates to Thurstaston Hall, what a place! Thurstaston Hall was recorded in 1070 'Levenot or Leofnoth' held it, Leofnoth held it in 1086. Thurstaston Hall was given to Robert de Rhuddlan by Hugh Lupus; the Thurstaston blood line came from the Norman ancestors of Mathew de Roelent. The Whitmore's held the Hall from the 13th century to 1751, when Joseph Whitmore died, thus ending over 500 years of the Whitmore's association with Thurstaston Hall.There were many attempts to lay claim to the hall, but none prevailed.

T H Mortimer described a moated site in 1847, the central part of the hall dated '1680 WWD' perhaps referring to restoration work! The west wing is 14th or 15th century and the east wing dates from 1835.The Tithe maps record the hall as owned by John Baskervyle Glegg.
A statue of the Earl of Chester was reputed to have stood in the Hall, a cutlass of Oliver Cromwell was owned by the family. On the death of Joseph Whitmore it was stated that he left it to his son-in-law, John Ignatius Wright.

As with most old buildings there is the enigmatic ghost; a lady is reported to haunt one of the bedrooms. A well-known artist stayed in the hall and allegedly witnessed the apparition; a lady ringing her hands in distress, the artist sketched the ghost which it was said to resemble a family likeness to the ancestors of Thurstaston Hall!

In 1971 workmen stumbled across a tunnel while laying a new water pipe outside the hall, the tunnel led from Thurstaston Hall towards Dawpool half a mile away. Was it used to avoid the customs men at Dawpool? What tales this house could tell if only walls could talk!

Now turn towards Station Road, the ground on the right belonged to the Gleggs during the 1800s, in 2009 permission had finally been granted to build a roundabout at the top of Station Road, there had been quite a delay in granting permission as, it was difficult to prove who owned the land. Now trees have been dug up and ditches dug, not as destructive as the 'Cut' during Ismay's time though. A house and garden stood at the bottom of the field in 1847, no sign of any buildings now though.

Before the journey back to the coast, take a walk to Thurstaston common. Walk to the junction of Station Road, cross the A540 and turn left, just after the Cottage Loaf pub is a small National Trust car park. The Cottage Loaf is a nice place to stop, summer or winter, for a meal and a drink, coke if you're driving!

Thurstaston Hill is 300ft high the 2nd highest hill in Wirral, Heswall being 359ft. Thurstaston hill and common are a delight to walk; many peaceful hours walking have been spent here with my family as youngsters, you don't need a map just wander the many grassy paths and go where the desire takes you.

The common is now a National Trust Reserve. For saving the commons for future generations our thanks must go back to 1879 when steps were taken to 'unenclose' Thurstaston common to allow a place of relaxation for the people of Wirral. This was accomplished by Birkenhead town council in 1881, what remarkable foresight, and what good sense! The joint owners of the land at the time wanted to retain the enclosure, whereby parcels of land could be sold off in the future.

Wirral has been fortunate that many of its open spaces have been retained for the good of the local population, and its many visitors, by local borough councils, or they have been given as a gift by wealthy landowners.
There are numerous paths to wander around on Thurstaston Hill and common, when you reach its highest point, views of Wirral, Formby, Wales, and the Lake district on a good clear day are unsurpassed. Likewise on a blustery winter's day the seascape and the hills shrouded in mist is still to be reckoned with.

Gorse and heather cover most of the hill, but interspersed with grassy knolls, plenty of places for a picnic! You will know when you have reached Thor's Stone, it's a massive outcrop of sandstone set within a grassy amphitheatre. Large grooves have been worn in the rock by human feet and by the rain running in rivulets down the rock face. There is much graffiti on the rock, but looking beyond this it is an imposing place, a visit would not be complete without a climb to the top, take care the rock is very smooth and can be slippy.

Thor's Stone 2009

Thor's Stone as it is called, is of bunter sandstone, this isolated crop of rock has a legend suggested by Sir James Picton 1805-1889.The legend suggested that the homestead of the Norse god Mjollnir was here at Thurstaston, and when the god struck his hammer lightning bolts lit the sky.

Perhaps the Norsemen, who travelled from Ireland and settled here in Wirral, witnessed lightning strikes on the ridge of Thurstaston which could have given rise to the name Thurstaston. Or was it the name of a local Norse man 'Thorsteinns' who had a farm close by!

The most plausible explanation for this isolated rock; is the harder rock around Thor's Stone has been quarried away leaving perhaps the softer core. Maybe the sandstone for Thurstaston's church was taken from here?

Here in Wirral there are many Norse elements found in place names. The Norseman, Ingimund, tells of his departure from Ireland with a band of followers.

He landed first at Anglesey then in Wirral in the year 902AD after an agreement with Ethelflaaed Queen of Mercia. Their departure and settlement in Wirral is recorded in the Irish Annuals and the Welsh Chronicles.

Now climb back to the trig point and walk towards the Rugby field, the rocky path here allows fantastic views of the river with Caldy and the plain between.

The plain between Caldy Hill and Thurstaston Hill 2009

Look towards Caldy Hill with Stapleton Wood in the foreground, Thurstaston Hill drops down to a plain between the two hills, this decrease and then increase in elevation is caused by a downward slippage of sandstone between two fault lines.

The same fault lines run out under the River Dee and towards the Welsh coast, the entire ridge running from Caldy to Shotwick tilts and slips eastward.

The open plain you are looking over was once the proposed site of a ship canal which was to run from Dawpool to Manchester. Robert Stevenson completed the survey in 1825, the canal was to take craft of up to 400 tons.
Wirral's north coast saw further canal projects; by Thomas Telford, Robert Stevenson, John Rennie, and Alexander Nimmo between 1823 -1837.
Luckily for Wirral none came to fruition!

As you gaze out over the fields, each bounded by a hedgerow, the majority of which have not changed for over 200 years, some for a much longer period. One wonders what the landscape was like during the Iron Age, in 1946 a Flint 'barbed and tanged' arrow head was found here on Thurstaston Hill in a mole hill of all places. Moles have on a number of occasions been amateur archaeologists! Perhaps Iron Age visitors to Thurstaston stayed and became one of our ancestors, what a nice thought.

Now Thurstaston has been explored walk back down Station Road, Dawpool farm is on your right just a few yards over to the right in the fields is an old track which ran from Dawpool Hall to the coast were the Dee sailing club is now.
This was the site of Dawpool Port; Dawpool Deep was the best anchorage on the west coast of Wirral and was just off shore at this point. Dawpool ceased as a port in the early 1800s.
See **appendix 5** for Vessels in the Port of Chester 1740-1769, Dawpool and Parkgate ports recorded.

The field boundary which was between Caldy and Thurstaston ran through a dale with its brook emerging at the headland. The dale was filled in as a rubbish tip and now is part of the golf links, the stream now emerges out of a pipe on the shore, not a very fitting end for one so pretty in the past.

Now we are on the last leg of our journey towards West Kirby, then a stride out over the sands to Hilbre Island.

Thurstaston to West Kirby and Caldy Village 2¼ to 4¼ miles

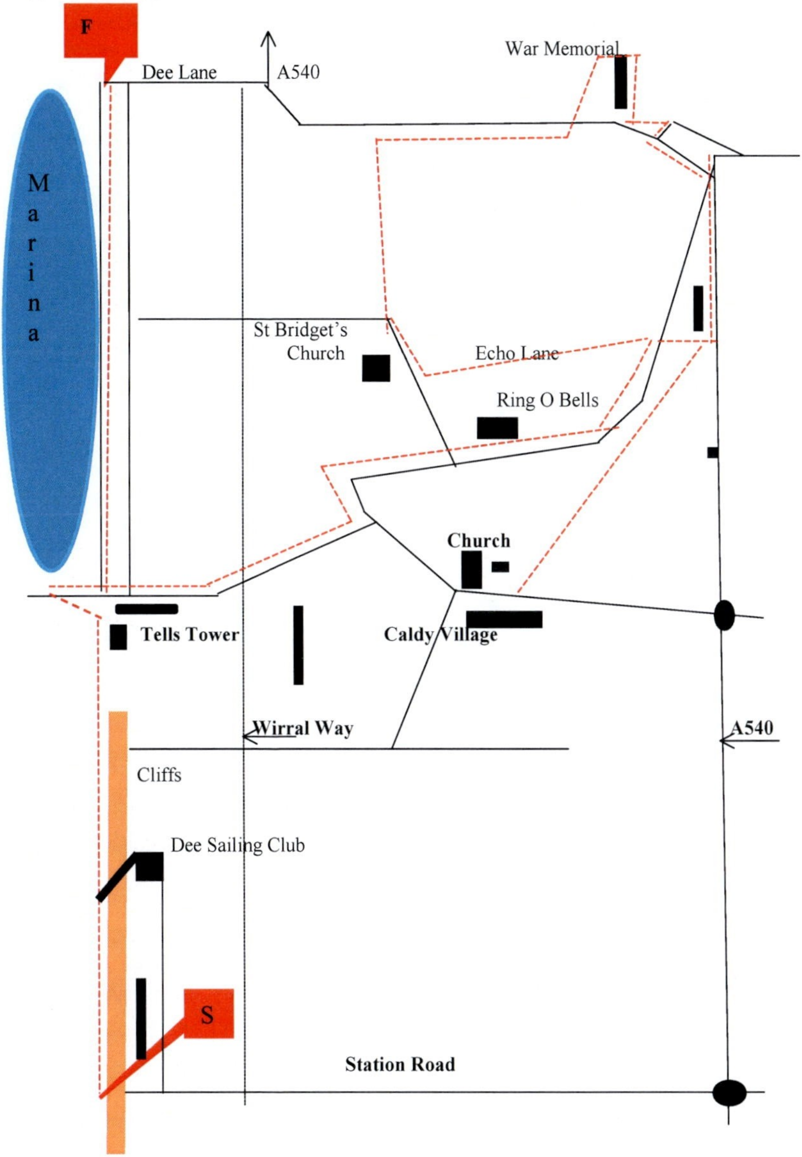

Chapter 15: Thurstaston to West Kirby

Check on the tides before you start this stretch of the walk, the sea meets the cliffs here and there is no way up the cliffs if you get caught by the incoming tide! The cliffs are recorded on some old maps as 'Redebonke' red bank due to the natural colour of the clay.

Slipway of Dee Sailing Club 2009

The slipway on the right leads to the Dee sailing club, with the coast stretching away behind you, ahead is West Kirby in the distance.
There is an old slipway out on the beach at this point; it's used for transporting boats to and from deep water channels off in the distance.

Many large sandstone blocks lie parallel to the cliffs about 20 metres off shore, in a north-south alignment. They are not linked but all follow the same alignment, many hundreds of smaller stones cover the beach in the vicinity of the larger blocks.

There are no known pictures of Dawpool harbour, but anchorage was well recorded on many old maps. The Gutter is quite deep, even at low tide boats are anchored here in deep water.
Recently during a winter storm two boats were torn from their moorings and were dashed against the rocks, which resulted in them no longer resembling boats, just flotsam!

At low tide Oyster Catchers probe the mud flats in search of food; a hawk flips overhead in search of his. Just below the golf course the boulder clay cliffs have slipped downward creating a two tier cliff line, cliff erosion has continued quite a pace over the last 100 years.

Large boulders have been used as a breakwater to prevent further erosion in this area; among the boulders is a large sandstone block, yellow-red in colour, not resembling those found on the beach.

The reason I noticed the stone; it had cement or plaster on all sides combined with a decorative pattern. One wonders where it came from; a fine building no doubt.

Caldy Beach looking towards Thurstaston Beach 2009

The cliffs are much lower here; West Kirby marina is in full view, the sandstone blocks which littered the shore a few yards back are now out of sight. Stone steps lead up to a car park at the bottom of Croft Road, a few more minutes and a footpath runs parallel to the beach up on the headland, it emerges on to Shelley Way.

Walking along the beach, on the right in a private garden is the remains of Tells Tower, a sandstone tower built in 1871-1874 by Reverend John Cummins McDona. The tower was built in the garden of Hilbre House to commemorate 'Tell' a Mount St. Bernard dog who drowned while trying to save his master on 22nd January 1871. The tower has been used for storage, a lookout post in World War Two and has been used by the Girl Guides; you can even find it on the Ordnance Survey map!

The last few yards along the beach is quite muddy, stay close to the wall its better under foot, at last here we are at West Kirby, all the way from Saughall. There is a wealth of history to soak up here, it's also a very pleasant place to while away a few hours; walk the marina, spend some time looking around the shops, relax.

In Caldy and West Kirby there is plenty to offer the visitor, fine views, plenty of good walks, a wealth of historical information; in West Kirby there are many good places to eat and drink.

Chapter 16: Great Caldy, Little Caldy.

Caldy was a minor 'Hundred' of Wirral in 1182 and was attached to the Manor of Gayton, the Doomsday Book recorded Caldy as having:
3 hides paying Geld
10 ploughs
5 villeins
5 bordars with 2 ploughs
1 Frenchman with 1 seviens (servant) with 2 ploughs in desmense and with 2 Oxen.
Caldy was worth 50 s after 1066 in 1087 it was worth 10s.

Caldy for its size was quite wealthy in terms of good plough land, *Robert of Rhuddlan holds Caldy, Leonoth held it before that; Robert also held Wallasey and Meols.*
'*Calday Parva and Calday Magna'* as they were known at the time the Doomsday Book was written, 'Great Caldy and Little Caldy'
Ergnent held Little Caldy; he was a free man it had 1 hide paying tax, land for 3 ploughs.
In lordship with 1 smallholder its value was 5 shillings now 10 shillings.

The 260ft Caldy ridge has Stapleton Wood at its southern end and Grange at its northern most point, West Kirby is snuggled on the west side of the ridge protected from severe easterly gales. The area has been a nodal point for visitors for many hundreds even thousands of years.

The National Trust own 13 acres of Caldy Hill, footpaths crisscross the hill and pleasant walks abound.

Stapleton Wood was given to the public by William Olaf Stapleton upon his death in 1950, prior to this R.W. Barton bought Caldy Township in 1832 and set about renovating the buildings in his manor. It's now a very desirable place to live; the present church was built in 1907, the black and white building opposite the old post office was known as the 'reading room'.

Caldy Hill is considered the site of 'The Kneckyn' this is Old Norse, Cnocc is Old Irish. Another recorded name for Caldy was; Kald-eyjar 'cold islands, sometimes referred to as, Cald ears or 'cold arse'. Perhaps the reference is to the shape of Caldy and its Islands, or maybe to their exposed location!

Chapter 17: West Kirby

Our walk through West Kirby is an interesting one; let's start at the end of South Parade by the sailing club, walk up Sandy Lane, the road leads over the Wirral Way by means of an old railway bridge.

When you reach the road junction, turn left into Village Road, this is a conservation area and includes a number of old properties. Pretty red sandstone houses stand either side of Village Road; the houses on the right were at one time shops, a tea room and butchers.

Ring O Bells 2011

Walk on towards the Ring O Bells built in 1810, it replaced an earlier inn of the same name, the cellar is hewn out of the sandstone bedrock and is known to run under Village Road itself.
The inn is another good place to stop and take refreshment during your walk around West Kirby.

Mariners Beacon on Caldy Hill 2009

Walk on following the road round to the left, within a few minutes you see a footpath 'Echo Lane' on your left, cross the road to the right, steps lead up Caldy Hill towards the Beacon.

This area is a Site of Biological Importance, there are 70 such sites in Wirral alone, including Grange Hill, and Stapleton Wood. Caldy Hill is noted for its heath, heather, gorse, butterflies, and trees, woodland birds, insects and even snakes! So tread carefully.

This area once belonged to the Abbey of Basingwerk, a monastic site in Flint in North Wales. Caldy Hill was also the site of Grange Mill, it was destroyed during a storm in 1839 , the mill had a secondary use as a beacon for mariners enabling them to determine their location while out at sea. There was a petition drawn up after the loss of the mill, and in 1841 the trustees of Liverpool Docks built a new Mariners Beacon, a Doric 60ft column topped with a sandstone ball. Built from local sandstone the column dominates the landscape for many miles. At the base of the beacon is an old mill stone.

The land was owned by John Shaw Leigh, he gave the land as a gift, and also laid the foundation stone; the area was called locally Liberty Park. It was the last remaining 'commons'; it was set aside for '*the right of the local ratepayers to be able to quarry stone for house and road repairs'*.

The views from the ridge are lovely, the footpaths to the right lead to Stapleton Wood, if you keep to the high ground; then if you wish take the path down to walk around Caldy Village.

In 1840, a few hundred yards from the column, a number of British Funnery urns were disinterred from a nearby garden, three were undamaged others were broken during digging. All were turned with their mouths downwards very near the surface, all except one; this had been placed in a sunken space between the rocks. They were made of course clay, they had been fired and contained burnt bone, wood, ash and were decorated. They are now in the Grosvenor museum in Chester. These small pots so carefully placed by perhaps a loved one, high up on the hill looking westward with strong fresh winds to carry away the spirit of the departed! Not so removed from peoples actions today.

Just before we leave Caldy Hill turn right and walk down Column Road. Within a few minutes you reach the Water Works, bore holes having been sunk in 1877 and 1892. The site is still in active use, just beyond the water works is Fleck Lane and the small sandstone building you see is called Well House.

Chapter 18: To the War Memorial

From Caldy Hill turn left on to Column Road, cross Village Road, walk past St Michael's the converted barn on the left, when it's safe to do so cross Grange Road. Then take the next right onto Grange Old Road, the tall sandstone wall was part of the Abbey estate and was built by Philip de Grouchy, he came from Jersey to construct the sandstone wall around the estate and stayed in a small house in Darmonds Green. In 1924 the council bought the land from Abbey Manor Estate, and re-routed Grange Road to avoid the hazardous bends. The large pine trees that stand on Grange Road were once part of the garden of Abbey Manor!

On the right behind the sandstone wall is the home of the Sea Cadets. The footpath we need is to the left of the first property in Grange Old Road, next to a pair of metal gates across the driveway. At certain times of the year the footpath sign can be hidden by foliage, the path we tread is on sandstone bedrock, the path curves around, above the main road.
Then the path opens out onto a grassy path with bedrock showing at intervals and within a few yards another iconic monument stands before you, that of the War Memorial, a poignant reminder of lives lost during both world wars and conflicts since including the present conflict in Afghanistan.

Grange Hill War Memorial 2009

The setting here on Grange Hill was well chosen, quiet, serene, there for all to see and remember. There are many such memorials in Wirral not as majestic as this one perhaps but equally as important.

The views here are fantastic, the Irish Sea, the River Mersey, and North Wales. While Hoylake, Moreton and Leasowe rest on the level plain, Wallasey and Bidston sit atop on sandstone ridges.

The view from Grange Hill showing Leasowe Lighthouse in the distance 2009

On the horizon new Wind Farms can be observed, the nearest being on Hoyle Bank, then Formby and then further out towards Anglesey and the mainland of North Wales.

I wonder in times past did local people believe that windmills were unsightly, even if they did contribute to the economy, perhaps much the same as today's view on wind farms, or is the jury still out.

Leave the area now from a path behind the memorial with West Kirby on your right; follow the path past some seats some of which have the wood rotted away. Shortly you reach a sandstone wall on your right, turn right here, care should be taken, exposed bedrock can be slippy after rain, continue down the hill until you reach Grange Road.

Chapter 19: St Bridget's Church and Museum

Walking down Grange Road with Drummonds Green on your right, opposite there is a footpath called Carpenters Lane, walk down the lane, within a few minutes you reach St Bridget's Church. This area, and the church, was once owned by Robert of Rodelent (Rhuddlan), it was granted to him after the Norman Conquest, a grant confirmed this in a charter of 1081 by King William. Robert granted land, and the church at West Kirby, to the Abbey of St. Ebrulf in Normandy. In 1138 West Kirby, and the advowson of the church, was bought for 30 shillings by Abbott William of the Abbey of St. Werburgh in Chester. The purchase included the islands of Hilbre.

During the troubled reign of King Stephen, the Manor of West Kirby was seized by the Earl of Chester and granted to the Abbey of Basingwerk in Flint. The advowson was strongly contested, the monks of St Werburgh wanted to maintain their ancient rights, so much so that an armed encounter took place within the walls of the church, and the monks of Basingwerk were defeated. Legal proceedings followed but the Abbey of St Werburgh reclaimed possession until the dissolution of the monasteries.

St Bridget's Church West Kirby 2009

It has been suggested that a pre Norman Conquest building stood on the site of St Bridget's Church, the name has Celtic connections to the Norse-Irish settlement that was known to exist here in West Kirby.

A possible Saxon church was most likely to have been made from wood but many Saxon churches were made of stone and still stand, See **appendix 6** 'Anglo-Saxon Churches of England'.

Many churches were destroyed and rebuilt by the Normans; but not all were destroyed some were altered piece by piece incorporating them into a 'new church'.

Norse settlers arrived here in the 10th century; the climate was mild, sheltered by the western slopes of Grange and Caldy hills.

Kirby is Norse for Church settlement, West was added later to distinguish it from Kirby-Walea (Wallasey). A charter of 1081 confirms the existence of a church 'Cherchebia' in West Kirby but it was not recorded in the Doomsday Book. West Kirby today has its namesake in Iceland 'Vestri Kirk Jubges' its church too is dedicated to St Bridget.

People have worshipped here for over a thousand years, parts of the Vestry are of the earliest date being 14th century, the east wall 15th and 16th century and the tower is 16th century but built around an earlier structure. A major restoration of the church took place in 1869-70 and is as you see it now, many stones from antiquity were found during the restoration of the church. Obtain a pamphlet from the church, it provides great detail on all the finds including the famous Hogback stone.

The Hogback Stone in St Bridget's Church West Kirby 2009

The Hogback stone is located inside the church, wait for the lights above the stone to be switched on; the detail which emerges is fantastic, very beautiful. It's a tombstone representing a shrine circa 1000 AD; they are quite rare and very important, as it must have been for the person for whom it was made, a local dignitary perhaps? Interestingly the rear of the Hogback stone is just as beautifully carved as the front view.

Take a walk around the church, then make your way across the churchyard to the Charles Dawson Brown Museum founded on his death in 1892. Incidentally he was an ancestor of the writer Greg Dawson who has written many books on the Wirral.

Charles Dawson Brown was a cotton broker and a local benefactor who lived in Stone Hive in Darmonds Green. The museum contains rare fragments of stones and stone crosses that were found during the church restoration, and again a pamphlet found in the museum gives lots of detail. The museum is housed in the old school house built in 1847 and restored over the years enabling it to grow with the community.

The small museum contains stones that are dated from pre Norman, Norman, and post Gothic periods. A tiny stone coffin for a child circa 1125 was one of many artefacts found, a sad reminder of infant mortality.

Tiny Stone Coffin of a Child circa 1125 housed in the Charles Dawson Brown Museum 2009

There is also a wheeled brier used for collecting corpses from the shore and transporting them to the church, and a hand brier used for taking bodies into the church. A fascinating array of artefacts, carvings some still ornate while others fading away.

It has been suggested that the stonemasons who made the Hogback stone had a workshop at St John's in Chester, the craftsmen there made stone crosses which were also found in Neston and Bromborough. The Hogback stone is said to mark the grave of a Christian not a pagan, during the period 1000-1050 AD the date the Hogback was most likely cut, perhaps this was a period of calm and prosperity in Wirral.

Stone crosses and other symbols representing Christianity were made for the prosperous deceased. St Bridget was a contemporary of St Patrick born in 455AD in Ireland to a pagan father and a Christian mother. St Bridget founded a religious community at Kildare and became Abbess; she was remembered throughout the Celtic world and thus the church here at West Kirby was named after her.

Buried at the south wall of the church under a red sandstone slab is; *Johannes Van Zoelen* he died in 1689, he was most probably attached to the Duke of Scomberg's army who were camped at Meols, a year before William of Orange embarked on his expedition to Ireland and the subsequent 'Battle of the Boyne'.

Take the time to look around the church and museum there is a fascinating wealth of information there, the opening times are limited so check before you travel.

Chapter 20: St Bridget's to West Kirby Marina

Time to continue on our walk, leave the museum and walk back along a path at the side of the church wall, at the end of this path turn right, then through a gate. It is a short walk to a final gate before emerging on to Rectory Road.

Cross Rectory Road just before the road meets the junction of Village Road, there is a footpath called Echo Lane on the left. Go over a stone stile, it's worth a few minutes to walk up the lane, stone pillars stand at the entrance together with a stone stile, cobbles lead the way up this leafy lane.

Echo Lane Photo 2009

On the right an old metal gate with its railings upturned to the sky stands abandoned within the stone wall, the remains of enclosed land forgotten now as we pass by. Old trees stand either side of the lane; a large stone wall appears on the left with a doorway built into it, now a metal gate guards the entrance.

This area once belonged to Abbey Manor, opposite the doorway stands a stone gate post now forming part of the boundary wall. Look at the stone wall both sides of the lane - various methods of stone-walling are present, large irregular boulders, square cut stones - hewn stones all form the bases of the walls at their lowest levels. They change to more modern machine cut stones nearer the top of the walls, some of the stones have chisel marks some have saw marks, all weathered and worn over time, they give an insight into the past of this leafy lane.

When you arrive at Village Road, turn right, walk on past the Ring O Bells and the thatched cottage called The Nook, and then retrace your steps back to the promenade. Walk down the promenade, on the left is Marine Lake built in 1899 at a cost of £2500; it has been extended and renovated a number of times over the years.

It's a pleasant walk around the lake; caution is needed as high tide covers the walkway.

The lake is a favourite place for wind surfing, yachting and, dinghy racing, watched by many people sitting or walking along the promenade on a winter's day or summer afternoon. Mind you, it can be hard to find a parking place any day of the week!

Sunset over West Kirby Marine Lake 2005

Where the promenade widens towards the lake, was the location of West Kirby bathing pool, now long since gone. Opposite the site of the bathing pool, where the apartments are now, stood the Hydropathic Hotel later renamed the Hoylake Hotel. The hotel opened in 1890 and was demolished only in 1960; it was a very popular place to visit in bygone days.

West Kirby is a very popular resort for local people and visitors alike. Good transport connections bring visitors from afar, there are numerous shops, restaurants, cafes, supermarket to provide needs for most people.

A walk out to Hilbre Island is breathtaking. When the tide is out there is a steady stream of people walking out to Little Eye winter or summer; they look like tiny ants crossing the sand! When walking out over the sand to Hilbre, it's important to check the tide tables, never walk out on an incoming tide.

Hilbre to Red Rocks a walk of 7 ¼ miles

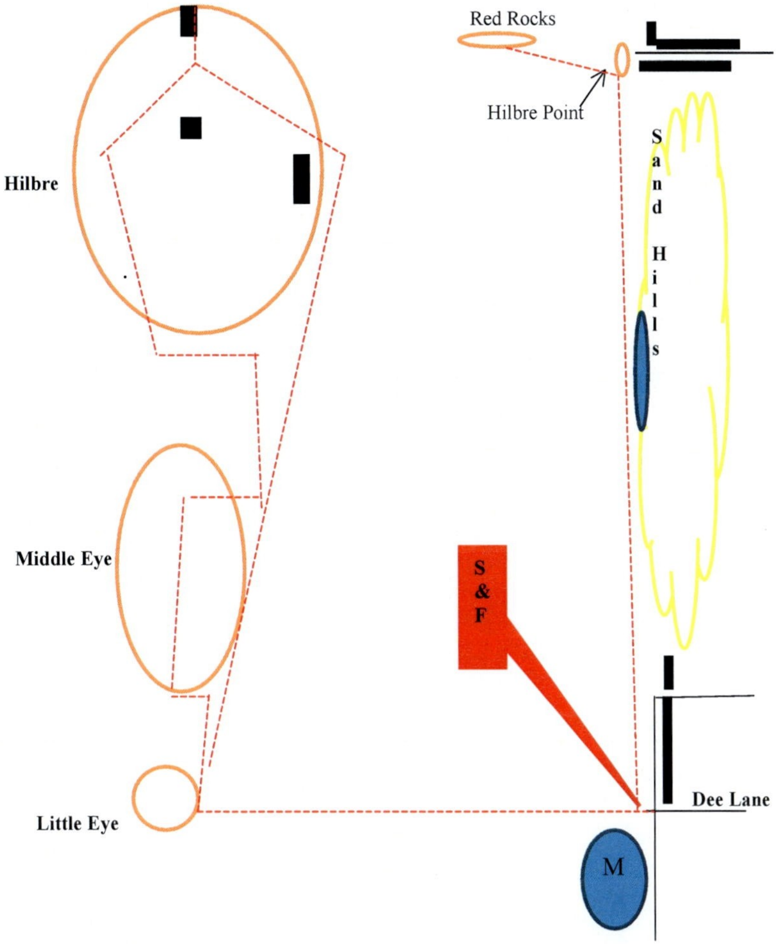

Chapter 21: Hilbre, Middle Eye and Little Eye

Hilbre Island 2010

Hilbre Island is13.5 acres, the largest of the three tidal islands situated at the mouth of the River Dee estuary. Middle Eye is 5.5 acres and Little Eye only .05 of an acre.

The islands are designated as a local nature reserve and a Site of Special Scientific Interest; they are only accessible by foot across 2 miles of sand from Dee Lane in West Kirby.

Never cross to Hilbre from Red Rocks in Hoylake.
The islands are cut off from the mainland for up to five out of 12 hours a day; if you decide to visit you must find out the times of high water. Allow yourself plenty of time to walk across the sands; the only safe route you can use is:

Walk from the Dee Lane slipway to Little Eye, then to Middle Eye, then on to Hilbre, at three hours after high water, and then the return trip must be started no **later** than three hours before high water.

Allow yourself longer if you are with small children, if there are strong winds, or if high water is over 9.5metre, all of these points can affect the time it takes to walk over the sands, and for the incoming tide to quicken its arrival.

History of Hilbre

Hilbre Island has had religious connections from at least the 7th century; St Hildeburgh Eye[island] or St Edburge was thought to be a 7th century Mercian Saint whose name was given to the island. The island was so named after Hildeburgh, and over the centuries the name became abbreviated to Hilbre. Was Hildeburgh alone when she went to the islands to spend time in solitude and prayer? Did she leave anything behind as a token of her stay? We may never know.

In 1066 Hilbre Island was part of the Manor of Caldy and was held by an Englishman named Leofnoth. After the Battle of Hastings William the Conqueror gave the Manor to Hugh Avranches who then passed it to Robert of Rhuddlan. Then in 1081 Robert gave the Manor to the Abbey of St Evroui in Normandy, in 1140 the islands were given to St Werburghs in Chester.

More changes of ownership followed:
In 1538 the islands were given to Chester Cathedral.
Then in 1856 the Mersey Docks and Harbour Board bought the islands.
In 1945 they were sold to Hoylake Urban Council for £2500.
Then in 1974 Wirral Borough Council bought the islands.
It was only in 1990 that full public access to Hilbre Island was granted prior to this you required a permit to visit!

In 1232 to 1237 John le Scott 8th Earl of Chester endowed a light to be lit by two monks on Hilbre, he gave 10 shillings a year for the light to act as a beacon for ships entering the Hoyle Lake. The endowment continued to be paid up to the dissolution of the monasteries!

In 1360 Trialbaston records in Chester record that a monk named Ranulf de Chaddesden from the cell on Hilbre Island, was charged with striking William de Bache with his fist in West Kirby two years earlier! In 1491 and again in 1498 John Lancaster, also a monk, was charged with striking someone.

There was a chapel on the island dedicated to the Virgin Mary and in the 1300s pilgrimages were made to '*Our Lady of Hilbyri'*. The islands were leased to Thomas Birkenhead on 10th September 1538 for a period of 61 years, the annual rent was 53s 4d, this included all of the islands and tithes of West Kirby, Irby and Woodchurch. 21 monks from St Werburghs signed the lease agreement; this was only weeks before the Abbey became Chester Cathedral!

In 1530 John Leland spoke of 'celle *of Monks of Chester* and *of pilgrims to Our Lady of Hilyri.*'

In 1539 Robert Harden, a monk, left Hilbre and became a priest at West Kirby St Bridget. Sir Robert Wiggan, 'clerk', of Hilbre left a will in 1550:
He was to be buried at St Bride [Bridgets West Kirby] He left bedding to his sister, a 'bote' called a Pyckerd named Michael of Hilbre, a brass pot, 'Redd Heyfar', Filly Calves. The last item in his will was a *gown morter.*

Robert Wiggan was an elder at the dissolution of the monasteries, and he retired to Hilbre and lived on a pension and supplemented this by fishing and farming. Robert was the senior of the two monks who lived on Hilbre, he died there in 1550.

Hilbre Islands consist of Bunter Sandstone of the Triassic period 180-225 million years old. The ridge of sandstone continues beyond the south of the islands and can be visible at very low tide. These rocks are known as Tanskeys, a possible Norse name; [*tonn* a tooth *Sker* a reef and *eye* for small island]. Seldom Seen Rocks and Caldy Blacks belong to the same outcrop of rock as Tanskeys. These rocks are located in the River Dee.

The cliffs on the islands have varied fault lines, some show pebble beds containing fossils. In the 1990s a fossilised footprint of a Chirotherium was found on Hilbre, it's kept in the Telegraph Station and can be viewed when the building is open.

The islands landscape dips towards the east with the higher cliffs on the west, the east side of the islands are therefore sheltered from the worst of the weather which provided a safe harbour for many hundreds of vessels over the centuries; it was known as Hoyle Lake.

7500 years ago the islands are thought to have separated from the mainland, due to the sea level rising when ice from the massive ice sheets which covered Britain and Europe were melting.

Over the millennia there have been many visitors to these islands, and they left behind many of their day to day items that we find extremely important.
Flint arrowheads and scrapers were found on the islands which show Neolithic man came here.

A Mesolithic layer where flints have been washed out from under the cliff has been identified.

A Bronze Age socketed axe was found and a fragment of a bucket shaped Urn.

An Anglo-Norse cross head was found in 1853, a Norman Cross head has been found also Anglo-Saxon beads were found on Hilbre, plus shards of Roman pottery.

A double ring cross, shards of pottery from the 3rd and 4th centuries. Medieval pilgrim tokens from the 13th and 14th centuries, pilgrims gave offerings to each shrine they visited some as far away as Santiago de Compostela in northern Spain.

Bronze brooches and buckles, 11th and 12th century grave slabs the list is endless.

A small cairn on Little Eye marked the resting pace of a person found in a crouching position. For such small islands the history surrounding them is immense!

In 2002 the Museum of Liverpool Archaeology team began a dig on Hilbre Island, their work concentrated on the eastern boundary wall of the gardens above the cliff top, erosion on this part of the island was giving cause for concern.

To Hilbre and its Islands

Follow in the footsteps of thousands, day trippers, seafarers, pilgrims, smugglers, even armies waiting to go to war, all travelled over the sands to Hilbre.

Little Eye's 'face' 2010

It's a 15 minute walk at a steady pace to reach Little Eye, the ripples in the sand change in intensity the nearer you get to Little Eye. A tall pinnacle of sandstone mixed with cement sits askew as though ready to tumble. Look closely at the right hand profile of the rock it resembles a face!

This northern landmark was used to guide ships through the sandbanks to Wales; the southern landmark was removed in the 1830s.

Little Eye 2010

Little Eye is a tiny hummock of windblown sand, some turf clutches with tenuous roots to the sandstone bedrock with barely any soil to speak off.

Little Eye is never fully covered by the tide unless heavy seas and strong winds lash its shore.

Looking out over the expanse of sea, wind farms are now part of the scenery. At the time of my visit to Little Eye the turbines on Burbo Bank were being repaired. The massive rig sits amongst the slender turbines almost obscuring some of them in the process.

Burbo Wind Farm 2010

The exposed sandstone bedrock surrounding Little Eye contain many rock pools, complete with tiny star fish, sea anemones, crabs and limpets all competing for space in their own world within a world!

To the right of Little Eye stretches a rock platform all the way to Middle Eye, to the left and in front of the island stretch the sandbanks of the River Dee estuary.

An unusual account was recorded in the early 12th century concerning these sandbanks:
Richard Earl of Chester '1101-1120' was a pilgrim on his way to St Winifred's Well in Holywell. Fearing he may be caught in a trap whilst staying at the Abbey of Baskingwerk, he sent a messenger to Chester requesting William Fitz-Nigel 'Constable of Chester' to bring the army, with all possible haste. Fitz-Nigel did as requested and made his way via Wirral to Hilbre, then seeking boats to cross the river he could find none. A monk from the cell on Hilbre suggested to Fitz-Nigel to pray to St Werburgh for assistance. On doing so their prayers were answered, a new sandbank rose up allowing the constable to cross the estuary into Wales and thereby assist Richard to return to Chester.
Richard was later to drown on 25th November 1120.

While researching for this book another curious record was found;
In the spring of 1927 the morning tide failed to arrive, it had reached Hoylake but no further!

Studies had shown, that on the previous day when a severe gale out in the Irish Sea was followed by a violent change in wind direction, it was thought that this could have been enough to create an oscillation; thereby holding back the tide! Perhaps this same phenomenon occurred when Fitz-Nigel was at Hilbre in 12th century! These sandbanks where known as 'Constable Sands'

Don't be tempted to cross the sands only danger lurks there; our walk is to Middle Eye.

The rocky plateau reaches out towards our next objective; the safer route to walk is along the sand to the right of the plateau. Shells, chert, flint, and stones of all shapes and sizes litter the beach; the view to Red Rocks and Hilbre Point is outstanding.

As you approach Middle Eye, cross the rocky beach onto the semi-circular sandy bay of the island.

Middle Eye 'Looking towards Formby' 2010

Red and yellow sandstone cliffs are the backdrop of the bay; natural arches have been cut into the cliff by wave action over millennia. Steps have been cut into the rocks on the left; these lead you up on to the cliff top.

The west shore of the island can be difficult to walk over, the rocks are covered with mud and seaweed coupled with numerous rock falls that have occurred; this area is best avoided.

Walk up the steps on to the grassy knoll which is Middle Eye, keep clear of the cliff edges there are many overhangs which can be dangerous. Look out over the sandbank towards a green buoy 'HE4' on West Hoyle Bank; here you will see a colony of Atlantic Grey seals. The seals haul themselves up onto the sandbank when the tide is low; there on the sandbank they bask in the sun out of the worst of the weather. The seals had been in decline a number of years ago but now their numbers can reach up to 500.

Below the cliff on the west coast of Middle Eye is the remains of 'Devils Hole' a tall thin cave, rock falls in this area have reduced the size of the cave, it was allegedly used by smugglers.

Nearing the end of the grassy plateau on Middle Eye are two upright rusty metal posts erringly sited at the edge of the east cliff. The route down to the rock platform below is to the left of the rusty posts.
Hilbre is only a few hundred yards from Middle Eye, the walk can be slippy at first over the rocks, golden sand spills out from Hilbre to make the walk a little easier!

The walk from Little Eye to Hilbre is nearly a mile in length, but you may have walked much further by your wandering hither and thither.

Approach to Hilbre 2010

Rock pools by the thousand can while away many hours, it reminds me of a cartoon which was in the Daily Mirror many years ago called 'The Perishers' *The King crab and his followers looked up from their rock pool searching for the 'Eyes in the Sky'* we are those eyes.

The islands give a wonderful 360 degree view of sea and land. Looking over the Dee estuary the weather is changing by the minute, dark clouds whip up over the Clwyd Mountains then dissipate as quickly as they are formed. Later over these mountains heavy rain clouds form that don't disappear.

Once across the sandy beach Hilbre beckons, the route ahead is up the concrete ramp on the left, the shore to the west of Hilbre is littered with rock falls, mud and seaweed making it difficult to walk over.

Below the west cliff there is a cave called Lady's cave, it has a rather sad legend associated with it. There are two versions of this legend:
One of the monks living on the island found a dying maiden washed up by the tide near the cave, with her last breath she told the monk of her plight, She was the daughter of the custodian of Shotwick Castle, against her father's wishes she fell in love with a young squire. The maiden's father informed his daughter that she was to wed Llewellyn a Welsh chieftain, the father put his daughter onto a boat to take her to her betrothed. The boat was lost at sea and the maiden swept onto Hilbre by the tide.

The second version:
A maiden was washed on to Hilbre by the tide a monk living on the island found the dying girl, she told the monk her story. While on a boat taking the maiden to her betrothed she informed her father that she loved another, not the man he had chosen for her. Her father did not approve, he informed his daughter that the man she loved had died; shocked by the terrible news she fainted and fell overboard. Her father was in despair, the maiden died in the presence of the monk.

Now on Hilbre our feet are on terra firma, the retaining walls alongside the concrete path were built in the 1890s by masons working for the Mersey Docks and Harbour Board.

On the left is a pond ,just past this on the right are three private wooden houses built between 1890 and 1920 by local families. The third house is used by the Hilbre Bird Observatory; the mound on the right in the middle of a small field was an air raid shelter and a generator room during World War Two. Lights on Middle Eye were powered from this generator, they were a ploy to detract German bombers from Liverpool docks.

In the fenced paddock on the right, a medieval grave slab was found in the 1860s, it is now in the Charles Dawson Brown museum in West Kirby. Nearby a Saxon-Norse cross head was found, this is now in the Grosvenor museum in Chester.

Original location of Theodolite and new technology 2010

A little further along the path, a Theodolite stood, it measured the height of the sandbanks out in Liverpool bay; now the Theodolite is redundant as modern technology uses satellites.

Careful near the edge of the cliff, rock falls can occur, next on the path is the Telegraph Station, a semi-circular white building with glazed windows.
The objects seen in some of the window panes are where binnacles were housed to support telescopes. The building was built in 1841 by the Trustees of Liverpool Docks; prior to the station being built a Semaphore system was introduced in 1827 to carry messages from Holyhead to Liverpool.

In 1856, electric cable was placed over land and across the Rivers Dee and Mersey to provide an improved communication system from Holyhead to Liverpool. The cable under the Mersey created numerous problems; it was constantly being caught by ships anchors!

The telegraph keeper in 1841 was Thomas Mathews aged 45, together with Elizabeth 25, Amelia 4, Thomas 2 and Henry 4 months.
Also living on the island was the mariner and Buoy attendant, Stephen Barnett aged 35 with his wife Mary Ann, there 3 children and farm labourer Mary Hewitt.

Telegraph Station on Hilbre 2010

In the third dwelling on Hilbre lived farm labourer Elizabeth Evans, Edward [Mulrooney], and five stone masons:
John Parry aged 40, Joseph Captree 30, William Captree 20, Edward Taylor 30, William Terfield 35; James Hignett 25 was a labourer.

To the rear of the Telegraph Station is a flight of wooden steps leading up over the station, the uninterrupted views from the top are fantastic. The turf is soft underfoot, and there are a couple of seats here which makes the area ideal for picnics and is shielded from the wind. When the Telegraph Station is open you can go inside, there is a cast of a dinosaur footprint there.

The white mast on the left is a solar powered navigational beacon, erected by Trinity House who are responsible for managing lighthouses in England and Wales.

The track we take is now downhill, over a tiny stone bridge spanning a gulley which stretches out into the sea. It won't be many years hence before this gulley cuts this part of the island off from the rest of the island.

Bridge over a gulley Hilbre 2010

There is a second bridge over a gulley, there is also what looks like a grave cut into the rock, but no, it was the base for a landmark system set up to alert shipping of the dangers around the islands. Now before you are the remains of Hilbre lifeboat station built in 1849 at a cost of £1200. Lifeboatmen were originally alerted to duty by two canons. After 1890 rockets were launched, even as a child I can readily recall three maroon rockets 'parachute flares' were launched to call the lifeboat men to action.

The picture on the right depicts the canon circa 1900.

The same view in 2010 where the canon once stood now stands a shed!

Hilbre lifeboat was used at low tide by the crew of Hoylake lifeboat station, the crew rode over the sands to Hilbre and the boat was then launched into deeper water.

The telegraph keeper would open the large wooden doors of the boat house ready for the crew to climb aboard the lifeboat, ship the oars and set sail to begin their rescue.

Metal rails were embedded into the floor of the slipway; this assisted the lifeboat to slide down to the water's edge. The marks are still visible on the ground where the metal rails once ran.

Lifeboat men on Hilbre before 1938. Notice the rails in the floor
Photo 'West Kirby to Hoylake' by Pat O'Brien.

The lifeboat station here on Hilbre was last used in 1938; this was due to the purchase of a diesel tractor which enabled the Hoylake lifeboat to be launched directly onto the sands from the mainland.

Walk through the doorway of the old lifeboat station, on the left is an old fireplace. Up above holes left in the walls are from long removed beams. To the right a tall window recess faces towards the mainland.

Inside the old lifeboat station on Hilbre 2010

A tiny station, what stories could it tell of the people who passed through its doors, blackened clouds overhead, howling winds, and with rain lashing its walls. The doors of the lifeboat station open, the boat travels down the slipway, aboard are her crew ready to rescue those in peril. Nothing but admiration to past and present lifeboat crews were ever they may be.

Hoylake lifeboat returning to base in March 2010

Walking down the sandstone ramp there is hardly a gap between the blocks, on the right hundreds of large sandstone blocks litter the sand and bedrock beach, all now exposed at low tide.

Old lifeboat station on Hilbre 2010

To the left is a large deep channel cut through the bedrock, it continues to the rear of the lifeboat station where the automatic tidal gauge is located. The gauge operated by the tide gives the height of the tides for the Port of Liverpool; it has been in operation for 130 years!

Just where a step crosses the channel, immediately in front of you on the rock face, is a wood tidal gauge with inscribed height markings. In the channel itself are more height marks etched in stone this time.

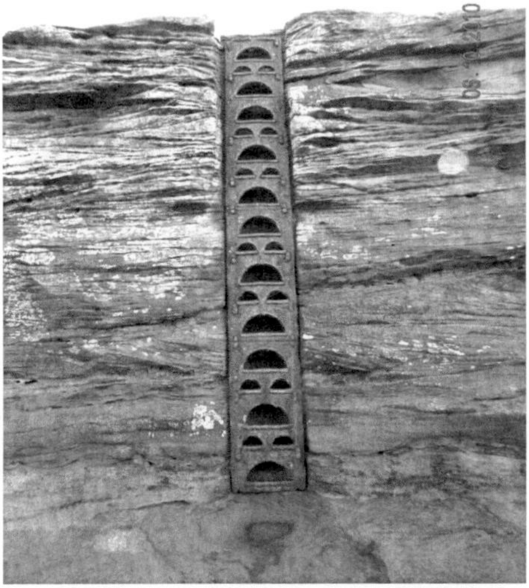

A few feet around the corner of the cliff face is a rusty ladder fixed into the cliff face; it was used by divers to reach the rock plateau below.

My father worked for the Mersey Docks and Harbour Board in the late 50s and early 60s; during this period he was called to Hilbre on many occasions with a diving team to assist in repairs to the tidal gauge.

Ladder adjacent to the lifeboat station on Hilbre 2010

The repairs were usually carried out during stormy weather or after a major storm, boat trips to Hilbre and on the River Mersey were not welcomed; as my father never learnt to swim even though he was in the Royal Navy during World War Two.

Mersey Docks and Harbour Board diving team 1950s, my father Archie Prince, is the third from the left on the back row..

Cliff face next to Hilbre's old lifeboat station 2010

The bedrock plateau stops abruptly and the cliff drops straight down to the rocks below, there is no access to the beach from here.

Now return to the lifeboat statio[n] and walk back up the path towards the Telegraph Station, the green wooden building on the left was built in 1900 by the Mersey Canoe Club; they still use the facilities here on Hilbre.

To the right of the building is a small slipway, we will venture there in a few minutes.

Across the grass you can see the rear of Telegraph House the white building with the tall chimney. The house was built in 1841 to house the telegraph keeper and his family; on the island they would have kept a horse or pony and cart for transport. Perhaps a pig, chickens sheep and a cow, even corn was grown at the south end of the island.

Next to Telegraph House was the 'Seagull Inn' or Beerhouse as it was sometimes known; first recorded in 1793 it was said of its patrons in 1813 that they made their fortunes from wrecking. Many hundreds of local inhabitants did the same all along the coast of Wirral.

There was also a customs house on Hilbre. Most probably the inn, over the centuries the leeward side of Hilbre was used as a safe anchorage, it was known as 'Hoyle Lake'. Ships would take advantage of this safe harbour as even during low tide there was always deep water at the western end of the lake. In 1571 10 ships were anchored at Hilbre and one at West Kirby.

Trade with Ireland prospered, cloth, coal, knives, sugar, raisins and pepper were transported to Dublin, the return cargoes were hides bound for the flourishing leather industry that Chester was enjoying.

Many armed troops made their way to Ireland from Hilbre, sadly, one would image that not all returned.

The Seagull Inn must have witnessed many a drunken brawl. It kept passengers fed and warm while waiting for a safe crossing to Ireland. The Inn finally closed its doors in the 1820s.

Many bodies have been washed up on Hilbre's shores, the eldest being Mary Corf aged 92 found dead on the beach in May 1821.

Below Telegraph House and the adjacent Buoy store is believed to be the site of the Saxon monastic cell, and the later medieval Benedictine cell. Monks continued to live and pray here on Hilbre until the dissolution of the Monasteries. Four skeletons were found on the island in the 19th century, they have not yet been radio carbon dated. One wonders who they were and when they died.

Return now to the slipway near the green hut, toilets are located just before the slipway. Down on the shore sandstone bedrock and sandy coves greet us, easy to walk over, not easy for young children though.

South view of Telegraph House and the Seagull Inn 2010

There is a good view of Telegraph House, Seagull Inn and the Buoy store from the beach. At the top of a flight of steps is where two canons were situated during the early 1900s, shown on previous photographs.

The deep channel out across the sands fills quickly when the tide comes in, there is no safe way over to the mainland from here.

Part of the cliff has been rebuilt here with sandstone blocks to protect the properties above from falling into the sea. Deep gullies have been cut into the bedrock, the remains of the Salt boiling industry that began in 1692, refining rock salt brought from the Cheshire Salt Mines up the River Dee to Hilbre; here it was refined into granular salt. The trade vanished when the ships were prevented from approaching Hilbre via the Dee.

The netting on the cliff edge above is used for capturing birds, to identify and ring them before letting them free.

A good path stretches out on the beach; thousands of mussel shells litter the sand, there are good views of Middle Eye and the mainland from here. Deep ravines have been cut into the cliffs by wave action, they provide interesting exploration opportunities. Take care where the cliff overhangs, rock falls are ever present. The rocks at the base of the cliffs are bright orange at this point, as the height of the cliff increases the rock turns to a dark red.

There has been a large slippage of rock in this area, weathering action has created small natural arches and sea stacks in the rock.

The end of one such sea stack hangs by a thread and the base has been repaired with red cement!

The inverted cone shaped rock on the left has been repaired! Photo taken 2010

The sand on this part of the island varies in colour from white to red; no shells, then thousands of them; it makes for an interesting walk.

The view out to Red Rocks, Hilbre Point, the war memorial on Grange Hill, and the Beacon on Caldy Hill stand out very clearly. In the past mariners used the same hills, Hilbre and Red Rocks to determine where they were in the estuary even before the beacon was erected.

We arrive back at Middle Eye keep to the left of the island; a good path is evident over the sands. The beach is littered with Flint, Marble, Granite, Quartz, millions of broken shells, and fragments of pottery, who knows, perhaps, even arrowheads if you look closely.

Rock fall on Middle Eye viewed from the south of the island 2010

The cliffs on Middle Eye also have collapsed, deep gullies cut into the rock leaving plenty of places to explore. When I was young a permit was needed to visit Hilbre, so my trips to the islands consisted of visiting Little Eye and Middle Eye.

Along the beach there are pools of red water under the cliff, no it's not blood but water from the peat bed which covers the sandstone rock above.
There are numerous rock pools and sandy coves just waiting to be visited.
The warden uses this route along the edge of Middle Eye towards Little Eye and hence to the mainland in a land rover; in the past islanders would have used a horse and cart or just used leg power!

Once past Middle Eye, a good stretch out to Little Eye awaits, now you are totally exposed to sea breezes and the worst of the weather. Deep ridges in the sand indicate the prevailing winds and tidal flow. Sandbanks rise up towards the island and beyond; in the distant Cormorants rest on the sandbank their faces turned to the prevailing wind and the sun!

The next 20 minutes takes you back over the sand towards West Kirby. Whether you enjoyed an energetic walk, a scramble over the rocks, or a quiet walk just taking in the views and fresh air; this is what Hilbre can offer its visitors.

Chapter 22: West Kirby to Red Rocks

This is the last part of our walk along the west coast of the Wirral peninsular, from Saughall to Red Rocks, what a journey so far.

After a windblown journey over the sands to Hilbre Island, before us now is a quiet stroll to Hilbre Point and Red Rocks. Starting at the steps at the bottom of Riversdale Road in West Kirby walk along the beach bearing in mind high tide meets the wall here for a few hundred yards.

The boundary garden wall keeps out the worst of the weather from destroying the plants, just a few yards on a footpath leads off to Lingdale Road. Within a few yards the sand dunes begin, there is a higher route above sea level or keep to the sand if the tide is out; the steps on the right take you to the higher route all the way to Hilbre Point amongst the sand dunes.

Taking the shore route we can wander at will when the tide is out picking the way through mounds of sea grass and flotsam brought up by the last high tide. The dunes although high are protected from erosion by large boulders; the dunes form the seaward side of the Royal Liverpool Golf Club.
(Charles Dawson Brown was one of the founders of the golf club)

Another footpath leads across the golf links to Meols Drive, the marsh here is known as Red Rocks Marsh, and it's a nature reserve maintained by Cheshire Wildlife Trust. The fenced off area is a breeding ground for Natterjack Toads, they are very rare in Britain and is the only breeding ground in Wirral.

You will notice on the shore line that there are two parallel sand dunes; the most obvious are the dunes on the right. The slight rise on the left where sand and grass form, are the remains of past dunes, constantly eroded and displaced by the sea.

The marsh itself is fed by an underground pipe which drains the golf links across the dunes, Spartina grass grows on the beach, hopefully it will not be allowed to spread, or it may lead to another 'Parkgate'.

Reed beds on the foreshore and Marram grass on the dunes gives this place a classification of S.S.S.I, 28 acres of marsh and dunes are open to the public. An abundance of bird and animal life, not to mention over 50 species of flowers and plants here too.

It's a lovely spot here tucked away on a quiet corner of Wirral, with breathtaking views of Wales, Hilbre, Liverpool and Formby. All around are clear horizons and sunsets that the artist Turner would be proud of. With an ever changing sky this area has a lot to offer all who look for its beauty.

Walking along the beach, tree trunks lie discarded some distance from the high tide mark, no doubt left by the previous tide coupled with high winds.

Hilbre Point is not far now, Red Rocks, known also as Red Stones, even Arnold's Eye is a rocky plateau a few hundred yards out across the sands from Hilbre Point.

Hilbre Point 2010

As a child I remember the rocks being much larger, or so they seemed to a small child. Rocks were places to hide amongst, climb over, jump off, pretending to be pirates and smugglers amid the rocks searching for treasure.

Hilbre Point and Red Rocks in the 17th century was the most southerly part of the Liverpool Custom Collectors area. It also marked the boundary of the English side of the River Dee, but as early as the 8th century England's land extended as far as Basingwerk near Holywell. Wat's Dyke marked the extent of political land grabbing in the 8th century, in fact Wat's dyke ran from Baskingwerk to Newbridge near Oswestry.

Red Rocks and Hilbre are classed as Triassic middle Bunter sandstone, the tidal platform at Red Rocks has produced prehistoric tool finds, over 20 pieces have been identified. These and thousands of other items are catalogued in a new book called 'Meols'. What a fantastic read for anyone interested in items of antiquity found here along Wirral's coast.

Today the rocks are partially covered by the tide; during the last glacial period global sea levels were much lower than they are at present. Glaciers depressed the Earth's crust, coupled with the water held in the ice the effect produced much lower sea levels. Once the ice began to melt the land mass rose and sea levels rose covering what was once dry land.

In prehistory the River Dee's estuary wasn't tidal; the coast ran much further out in the shape of an arc towards Morecambe Bay!

Studies are on-going at Red Rocks and Hilbre, settlement or human activity occurred periodically, perhaps seasonal at first, archaeological finds are few but significant.

This is the end of our journey from Saughall to Red Rocks, whether you walk it as one long walk or take weeks or years, the most important thing is the journey. We all take them through life, why not take your time, relax and enjoy.

My next journey will be from Hoylake to Eastham, following the coast as much as possible, then across country back to Saughall. I don't know how long it will take but I know I will enjoy every step of the way.

Hilbre Point taken from Hilbre Island 2010

Appendix 1

Chester Murage Roll 1441-1442

Cheshire Archives and Local Studies (Cheshire Shared Services) mur/1sti/144.

The above is reference to a Murage document which is held in Cheshire Archives, and has been transcribed and translated by the author Marilyn Stevenson.

The contents of the Murage document refer to Murage duties paid and collected; which in fact were the receipts of tolls taken at each of Chester's city gates; Northgate, Eastgate, Bridgegate and Watergate. It also includes customs duty paid on goods coming into Chester and was paid by the merchants of the city. The money collected was then expended on the repair of the city walls and the bridge at Bridgegate.

The document is on three pieces of rolled parchment, is written in Latin and the text covers both sides of the roll, this was a common method of storing information in 15th century.

The tolls were collected weekly from 13th December 1441 to 12th December 1442 in the reign of King Henry VI.

Bartholomew Lyalton and Johannus Copeland were 'Murengers' Collectors of tolls whose duty it was:
'To receive the murage tolls and customs duty and expend the same in repairs of the city walls and bridge'.

The tolls collected between the years 1441 to 1442 for each of the city gates was as follows;

Eastgate	£1	2s 10d ½
Bridgegate	£1	19s 5d ½
Northgate	£0	7s 11d ½
Watergate	£0	4s 10d ½

Watergate which led down to the River Dee was the least used of the city gates, where tolls had to be paid; this in part was due to the silting of the River Dee which caused major problems for the city's commerce even in the 15th century!

The following names are merchants of Chester who paid tolls and customs duty and whose names are recorded on the Murage Roll.

The spellings of the names are as shown on the original document.
[ ] *denotes possible spelling*

John Cotyingham of London
Jacob Freley
Richard Hawrden
Jacob Chalderton
William Walles
James Dokray
John Walmon
William Paynel
John Pentver
Robert Feles
John Blakelow
John Younge
Roger Goldsmyth
John Ludlowe
William Hocheynson
John [Telor]
John Bathe
David Childerton
Hugh Tetlowe
Robert Brode
John Savage
Richard Palmer
Thomas [Horfoyd]
[?] [Tompen]
John Garland
John Wetenhale
John Bon y Pente (Welsh perhaps!)
John Dale
William Bryan
[?] Stawagh
Richard White
John Blakin
Thomas Banceray
John Park
John Lucas
Thomas Harband
[?] Bronne or Brown
Thomas Tympenes
William Massey
Robert [Walshenlen]

Richard Bedlowe
Arnold Hosyer
Thomas Savage
John [Slabas]
John Skynner
John Hatis
Richard Goldsmith
John Matlay
[?] Ersteken
Philip Wetagur
Robert Baille
Thomas Wotham
John [Catur]
Thomas [Sp—r] de Clareley
John Darkin
John Selveste
Thomas Savage
John Erstken
Richard Palmer
Thomas Herband
John [Yongi]
John Irell

John Asser senior, was appointed Master Mason for Chester and Flint in 1432. John Asser junior was appointed Master Mason for Chester and North Wales in 1438.

Including the tolls, customs duty was collected; the money went towards the cost of labour, tools and building materials for the repair of the city walls, gates and bridge.

The following names are merchants of Chester, who during 1441 and 1442 paid in money or goods towards those repairs:

John Minour and Henry Barbour were paid 6s 10d for timber used on the bridge.

Edward Skynner and John Herford were paid 6s 3d for timber used on the bridge.

John Layot was paid 5s for timber used on the bridge.

Richard Botyll was paid 7s 12d for the carriage of timber used on the bridge.

Thomas Coke and his son David were carpenters, they were each paid 2s 6d for their work on the bridge.

Richard Masson was paid 3s for stone and sand used for the repair of the bridge.

Miles Paver was paid 2s for work on the bridge.

The Dominican Friars were paid 6s for stone brought from the quarry at Halgh Green now known as Hough Green.

Thomas Hexham was paid 5s for stone.

Thomas Byley was paid 14d for 7 carts of sand.

William Doneham was paid 8d for the carriage of sand.

John Newton was paid 6d for the flooding of the road at the Westgate.

Robert [Woud] or Wood was paid 3d for 3 carts of gravel.

Mathew Masson and Hugh Masson were each paid 2s 6d for a day's work on the 'New Tower', the tower was built in 1322 at a cost of £100. It was built by John Helpstone and was known as the 'Water Tower'.

Henry [Waterladen] was paid 6d for stone for the 'New Tower' and 3d per day for 2 days work.

Adam Lokker was paid 8d for one lock for the door in the 'New Tower'.

Henry [Quarriour] was paid 4d a day for 3 days work as a quarry man.

John Henste was paid 18d for 1 week's work.

John Barbour was paid 18d for his work and the use of one cart.

Thomas Byley was paid 8d for 2 carts of stone and 1 of sand.

Robert [Woud] Wood was paid 6d for 2 carts of stone.

Miles Smith was paid 4d for paving outside the gate near Handbridge; he was also paid 40d for paving at the Eastgate.

John Bronne was paid 4d for pointing the same stones.

Anderson Smyth was paid 12d for sharpening and shaping of pick axes and wedges.

Jacob de Huyton was paid 13s 4d, he was a clerk.

John Asser charged a fee of £10 for his work on the walls and bridge.

There is so much to learn from such a document, what a fantastic insight into the lives of everyday citizens; their names and occupations, what they were paid for a day's work, the materials they used and even the method of transporting the goods.

It's a peep into the past, Chester's walls and bridge remain, the Murage document is very fragile but is secure for future generations to marvel over. The surnames listed, if you have an interest in family history, can take the reader back over 500 years, you may be lucky to find your name amongst them.

Most of all when you next travel to Chester take the time and walk around the city walls, visit the gates, bridge and Cathedral. Imagine the citizens going about their daily work nearly 550 years ago!

Appendix 2

Militia Book of Neston 1760-1766

Reference QA A6 Cheshire Archives and Local Studies (Cheshire Shared Services)

The following names are taken from the Militia Book of Neston dated 1760-1766; it records payments to wives and children of the Cheshire Militia living in Neston.

1760 Great Neston paid to Hannah Barlow 8weeks	£1.14.0d
1760 Great Neston paid to Mary Robinson 8 weeks	£1. 8. 0d
1760 Little |Neston paid to Sarah Johnson 7 weeks	£1.15.0d
1760 Little Neston paid to Sarah Johnson 24 weeks	£6. 6. 8d
1760 Great Neston paid to Hannah Barlow 20	£1.18.3d
1760 Little Neston paid to Sarah Johnson	£2. 0. 0d
1761 Great Neston paid to Hannah Barlow 28weeks	£4.13. 4d
1761 Great Neston paid to Hannah Barlow 12 weeks	£2. 0. 0d
1761 Little Neston paid to Sarah Johnson 13 weeks	£2. 3. 4d
1761 Little Neston paid to Sarah Johnson 16weeks	£2. 0. 0d
1761Little Neston paid to Sarah Johnson 15 weeks	£2.10. 0d
1761 Little Neston paid to J Johnson 10 weeks	£2. 0. 0d
1761 Great Neston paid to Hannah Barlow 38 weeks	£8. 2. 0d
1762 Great Neston paid to Hannah Barlow 14 weeks	£2.16. 0d
1762 Great Neston paid to Hannah Barlow 10 weeks	£2. 0. 0d
1762 Great Neston paid to Roberta Barlow wife 9 weeks	£1.16. 0d

For the years 1764, 1765, and 1766 no names are given, although a total of 13 payments were made.

Hannah was married to shoemaker Robert Barlow; they had seven children while living in Neston, Robert was born in 1728 his father was Joseph Barlow.

Sarah Gladwin married Thomas Johnson a farmer in 1759, they lived in Willaston and had five children born there. Witnesses to the wedding of Sarah and Thomas were W Bullock, and Eliz and John Wolstenholme, these were important members of the community at this time, all signed the marriage deed except for Sarah.

Delving into family history can lead to more questions than answers, but it is all consuming.

Appendix 3

Local Militia List for the County of Chester including the Sub Division of Wirral 1809- 1811.

Reference MF 210/4Cheshire Archives and Local Studies (Cheshire Shared Services)

The list includes balloted men and volunteers with their occupations; the list is shown as recorded in the original document.

Name	Village	Occupation
William Hughes	Hoose	Tailor
John Hesketh	Stanlow	Servant
David Trueman	Shotwick	Labourer
James Shone	Blacon	Servant
Samuel Hughes	Backford	Servant
George Shone	Blacon	Servant
David Catherall	Little Sutton	Smith
Charles [Crop]	Shotwick Park	Labourer
Samuel Read	Shotwick Park	Farmer
Samuel Jones	Shotwick Park	Servant
William Hayes	Raby	Labourer
John Smith	Thornton Hough	Servant
Hugh Randles	Thornton Hough	Farmer
George Taylor	Shotwick	Servant
Edward Taylor	Thornton Hough	Labourer
John Jones	Little Stanney	Labourer
Thomas Hill	Childer Thornton	Farmer
Charles Dakin	Childer Thornton	Tailor
Samuel Peacock	Childer Thornton	Farmers son
Richard Bird	Childer Thornton	Weaver
Richard Hall	Little Stanney	Servant
Thomas Meolse	Liscard	Servant
John Ashton	Thurstaston	Servant
Thomas Smith	Birkenhead	Farmer
John Pover	Tilston	Servant
John Barton	Liscard	Gentleman
John Williams	Eastham	Servant
William Hughes	Landican	Servant
Samuel Moore	Willaston	Joiner
Samuel Kendrick	Willaston	Servant
Charles Jones	Willaston	Servant
Joseph Bird	Willaston	Farmers son

Thomas Candleton	Puddington	Servant
George Disley	Puddington	Servant
Joseph Dunning	Wervin	Wheelwright
Joseph Smith	Woodbank	Servant
William Peers	Willaston	Servant
Robert Ellis	Brimstage	Labourer
George Edwards	Brimstage	Slater
Robert Venables	Bromborough	Tailor
Samuel Mellor	Bromborough	Farmers son
George Evans	Bromborough	Tailor
Thomas Owan	Brimstage	Farmers son
John Roberts	Burton	Servant
James Duncan	Burton	Labourer
Joshua Pulford	Burton	Labourer
Thomas Scoles	Burton	Labourer
Thomas Nelson	Heswall	Servant
David Whitehead	Burton	Mason
William Hough	Heswall	Farmer
John Rathbone	Burton	Tailor
Thomas Charnley	Overpool	Servant
Charles Hunter	Eastham	Labourer
John Malt	Eastham	Labourer
Samuel Joinson	Eastham	Labourer
Thomas Nicholls	Eastham	Labourer
James Davies	Eastham	Labourer
William Ashton	Eastham	Labourer
Thomas Baker	Christleton	Servant
Thomas Hancock	Eastham	Servant
John Ashton	Eastham	Labourer
John Walton	Lower Bebington	Servant
John Spark	Lower Bebington	Farmer
Charles Langley	Lower Bebington	Carpenter
John Woodfine	Barnston	Farmers son
William Bennett	Great Sutton	Servant
John Dutton	Great Sutton	Farmer
Thomas Hacney	Great Sutton	Servant
Thomas Burroughs	Great Sutton	Labourer
Richard Miller	Great Sutton	Servant
John Boscow		Farmers son
Thomas Youd	Arrow	Farmers son
Robert Carrington	Prenton	Farmers son
Thomas Baker	Christleton	Servant
Edward Peers	Prenton	Servant

Richard Hale (discharged unfit)	Greasby	Farmers son
John Lee	Greasby	Servant
Thomas Smith	Caldy	Farmer
Peter Philips	Grange	Servant
William Pownall	Grange	Weaver
John Jones	Thingwall	Labourer
Edward Price	West Kirby	Servant
Thomas Hindley	West Kirby	Farmers son
Henry Taylor	West Kirby	Farmers son
John Powell	Greasby	Servant
Thomas Lawrence	Mollington	Servant
William Bennett	Great Sutton	Servant
Thomas Hacney	Great Sutton	Servant
Thomas Burroughs	Great Sutton	Labourer
Richard Miller	Great Sutton	Servant
Thomas Wills	Hooton	Footman
George Worthy	Hooton	Butler
John Chamberlain	Upton	Servant
Thomas Washington	Great Meolse	Farmers son
Jonathon Potter	Saughall Massie	Farmers son
John Pulford	Netherpool	Servant
Thomas Davies	Newton	Servant
Thomas Spencer	Newton	Farmer
John Rainford	Newton	Labourer
James Jones	Woodchurch	Servant
Mathew White	Eastham	Servant
Thomas Jackson	Woodchurch	Servant
Samuel Bennett	Whitby	Labourer
Richard Hawley	Whitby	Servant
Jonathon Grimes	Broughton	Servant
Thomas Oakes	Chorlton	Farmers son
Samuel Blake	Chorlton	Servant
Thomas Tasker	Stoke	Servant
William Thomason	Lea	Blacksmith
James Bunnell	Stoke	Farmers son
John Grimes	Whitby	Servant
Samuel Benson	Whitby	Servant
William Bailey	Broughton	Servant
James Radley	Bidston	Servant
John Pendleton	Bidston	Farmers son
George Parr	Bidston	Servant
Robert Woodfine	Bidston	Joiner

William Kemp	Bidston	Servant
George Prince	Irby	Servant
John Totty	Irby	Servant
William Houghton	Irby	Tailor
William Jackson	Irby	Blacksmith
Samuel Trueman	Irby	Labourer
Joseph Jones	Irby	Servant
Samuel Ledsome	Storeton	Servant
Peter Jones	Storeton	Servant
Thomas Bell	Wallasey	Labourer
William Hayler	Wallasey	Labourer
Richard Joinson	Wallasey	Labourer
George Hayler	Wallasey	Tailor
Robert Youds	Frankby	Servant
James Philips	Frankby	Farmers son
Robert Little	Great Meolse	Farmers son
John Ley	Upton	Labourer
Robert Edge	Tranmere	Labourer
John Thomason	Tranmere	Servant
Samuel Johnson	Tranmere	Servant
George Davies	Tranmere	Labourer
Thomas Evans	Tranmere	Blacksmith
Richard Huxley	Aldford	Labourer
Thomas Pickstone	Upton	Cordwainer
Robert Allmark	Ledsham	Blacksmith
William Pritchard	Little Neston	Farmers son
William Lawley	Ness	Collier
Thomas Littlemore	Ness	Collier
Charles Glover	Ness	Bricklayer
John Jones	Ness	Collier
Samuel Littlemore	Ness	Collier
Thomas Duncan	Ness	Labourer
James Littlemore	Ness	Collier
John Parr	Ness	Labourer
Thomas Barton	Little Neston	Labourer
William Woodworth	Little Neston	Labourer
Natham Grimes	Great Saughall	Servant
James Acton	Great Saughall	Labourer
Thomas Rogers	Great Saughall	Servant
Charles Jones	Leighton	Labourer
Samuel Kenrick	Ness	Labourer
William Hughes	Great Neston	Mason
William Mathews	Great Neston	Joiner

Joseph Jones	Great Neston	Joiner
Thomas Hilsby	Great Neston	Cordwainer
Richard Hughes	Great Neston	Furrier
Hugh Williams	Great Neston	Joiner
John Washington	Great Neston	Labourer
Thomas Maddock	Great Neston	Butcher
John Pattison	Great Neston	Collier
William Ingram	Great Neston	Servant
John Mathews	Great Neston	Labourer
John Smith	Great Neston	Cordwainer
William Welch	Great Neston	Joiner
John Ashbrook	Great Neston	Labourer
Thomas Clayton	Great Neston	Cordwainer
Thomas Robinson	Great Neston	Cooper
Peter Parr	Great Neston	Farmers son
William Somerfield	Great Neston	Sawyer

Militia Roll
Royal Chester Regiment
1813 – 1815 including Wirral

Name	Age	Village	Occupation
William Hay	29	Backford	Servant
George Benson	28	Backford	Farmer
John Joinson	22	Eastham	Labourer
William Nelson	20	Mickle Trafford	Shoemaker
John Darlington	21	Backford	Shoemaker
William Richardson	29	Backford	Shoemaker
John Maddocks	18	Backford	Labourer
John Evans	18	Barnston	Servant
Robert Ainsworth	20	Barnston	Labourer
William Mainwaring	28	Liverpool	Tailor
William Owens	20	Barnston	Farmers son
Thomas Goodacre	19	Lower Bebington	Labourer
William Goodacre	20	Lower Bebington	Labourer
Richard Evans	18	Lower Bebington	Farmers son
John Millington	23	Poulton	Labourer
William Bradshaw	23	Lower Bebington	Slater
Edward Leather	26	Lower Bebington	Weaver
Thomas Goulson	19	Lower Bebington	Labourer
Robert Heney	27	[?]	Furrier
John Hazlehurst	28	Bidston	Labourer
Thomas Corf	28	Bidston	Labourer
John Smith	21	Bidston	Labourer
James Still	21	Liscard	Labourer
John Hendricks	29	Brimstage	Farmer
Joseph Polland	23	Brimstage	Tailor
John Langley	22	Brimstage	Farmers son
Edward Lloyd	19	Brimstage	Servant
William Clarke	21	Irby	Labourer
William Downham	21	Upton	Labourer
James Leather	18	Bromborough	Miller
William Leather	20	Bromborough	Labourer
George Ashton	20	Bromborough	Labourer
William Jones	25	Bromborough	Labourer
Edward Green	20	Eastham	Servant
Thomas William	23	[?]	Wheelwright
John Scholes	30	Burton	Labourer

Samuel Webster	20	Burton	Labourer
John Williams	30	Puddington	Labourer
William [?]	27	Burton	Coachman
George Mack	22	Burton	Cordwainer
William Williams	22	Burton	Labourer
George Pearce	19	Puddington	Labourer
William Joynson	19	Burton	Labourer
James Taylor	26	Bidston	Slater
John Grimes	23	Tranmere	Labourer
Richard Ledsome	22	Brimstage	Labourer
John Evans	21	Moreton	Servant
Thomas Leathers	22	Barnston	Shoemaker
John Dean	19	Woodchurch	Servant
Samuel Jones	19	Aldford	Servant
John Birches	31	Burton	Labourer
Thomas Cooper	21	Burton	Tailor
Enoch Ashton	18	Burton	Labourer
John Rathbone	26	Burton	Sadler
Thomas Kendrick	27	Newton/Larton	Husbandman
John Davies	23	Newton/Larton	Husbandman
William Mainwaring	21	Backford	[?]
James [?]	18	Neston	Servant
Thomas Otterhead	19	Neston	Cordwainer
Joseph Littlemore	23	Little Neston	Labourer
Thomas Hancock	19	Little Neston	Labourer
John Kendrick	18	Little Neston	Servant
Thomas Much	20	Little Neston	Servant
John Fairbottom	18	Ness	Labourer
Thomas Maylor	18	Little Neston	Labourer
Thomas Lloyd	23	Ness	Wheelwright
John Rowland	19	Puddington	Labourer
William Littlemore	21	Ness	Cobbler
James Burkill	19	Ness	Labourer
William Cotterall	21	Ness	Labourer
Joshua Pulford	20	Burton	Labourer
Samuel Johnson	28	Ness	Servant
Arthur Cartar	22	Thornton	Tailor
John Ball	23	Thornton	Labourer
John Pears	26	Thornton	Labourer
John Swift	21	Leighton	Butcher
Joseph Hughes	21	Leighton	Labourer
James Bartley	19	Leighton	Sawyer
Thomas Pears	20	Leighton	Labourer

Richard Williams	18	Raby	Labourer
Robinson Bennett	22	Wallasey	Farmers son
John Buckley	19	Wallasey	Tailor
William Davies	21	Wallasey	Labourer
William Kay	28	Wallasey	Wheelwright
Thomas Joynson	27	Bidston	Servant
George Totty	21	Irby	Labourer
George Allcock	22	Greasby	Servant
William Dixon	21	Little Sutton	Labourer
Joseph Calveley	23	Storeton	Farmers son
Thomas Grice	21	Storeton	Labourer
John Williams	23	Storeton	Labourer
Thomas Milner	20	Willaston	Labourer
Thomas Griffith	23	Willaston	Labourer
Thomas Maylor	21	Willaston	Labourer
Edwards Parr	19	Willaston	Labourer
John Mann	20	Willaston	Miller
Richard Davies	25	Little Stanney	Servant
Richard Wright	29	Little Stanney	Labourer
John Lewis	19	Ashton by Chester	Labourer
James Fairdon	29	Little Stanney	Servant
Edward Davies	27	Little Stanney	Servant
George Tomlinson	?	Stoke	Labour
John Catherale	18	Little Sutton	Blacksmith
John Hinley	20	Little Sutton	Labourer
Thomas Hughes	24	Bachford	Labourer
Samuel Moulton	20	Little Sutton	Shoemaker
John Hough	20	Great Saughall	Labourer
George Harrington	19	Great Saughall	Labourer
John Rosedale	25	Mollington	Labourer
Thomas Darlington	19	Great Sutton	Blacksmith
Thomas Lancely	20	Mollington	Labourer
Thomas Jones	23	Shotwick	Labourer
Samuel Bale	29	Little Stanney	Farmers son
John Roberts	23	Stoke	Servant
Thomas Wirral	20	Oxton	Labourer
William Hallewood	20	Oxton	Labourer
Peter Mellor	20	Great Neston	Cordwainer
Thomas Hanyan	24	Great Neston	Cordwainer
William Quigley	22	Great Neston	Cordwainer
William Price	19	Great Neston	Cordwainer
Richard Johnson	20	Great Neston	Joiner
William [B]	21	Great Neston	Slater

William Hanyan	18	Great Neston	Cordwainer
Thomas Maddock	22	Great Neston	Butcher
John Alderhead	26	Great Neston	Labourer
William Griffiths	19	Great Neston	Labourer
Samuel Jones	19	Great Neston	Collier
Joseph Gibbon	19	Great Neston	Farmers son
William Pritchard	25	Little Neston	Farmers son
John Smith	23	Great Neston	Tailor
Joseph Griffiths	20	Great Neston	Butcher
Samuel [B]	22	Great Neston	Collier
John Robinson	30	Great Neston	Collier
Daniel Oates	31	Great Neston	Labourer
Samuel Cowell	21	Great Neston	Labourer
Thomas Williams	19	Liverpool	Joiner
Edward Wilkinson	22	Hooton	Servant
Edward Robson	21	Hooton	Servant
Joseph Lloyd	24	Hooton	Labourer
John Leather	21	Wallasey	Servant
Stanley Dean	21	Liscard	Farmer
Joseph Corf	20	Liscard	Shoemaker
Thomas Griffiths	21	Liscard	Farmers son
Jonathon Dean	21	Liscard	Husbandman
Peter Croft	18	Bachford	Servant
Henry Boyse	31	Eastham	Servant
Edward Hamenisty	29	Childer Thornton	Servant
Thomas Warrington	19	Eastham	Labourer
John Ashton	19	Overpool	Servant
Daniel Washington	25	Eastham	Labourer
Peter Woodward	27	Eastham	Mason
George Roberts	21	Eastham	Blacksmith
Joseph Thelwall	21	Liverpool	Labourer
Thomas Catterall	21	Eastham	Labourer
Thomas Hughes	19	Bachford	Cordwainer
Henry Grace	21	Thurstaston	Farmers son
John Dod	?	Heswall	Servant

NB: [ ] denotes illegible writing, Names are in the same order as the original document.

Appendix 4

Petition of 1726 from Neston's Inhabitants

EDC 5/1/13 Cheshire Archives and Local Studies (Cheshire Shared Services)

On 16th July 1726 in Chester the Notary Publics; Johannus Carter and [Gal] Moulding heard a petition from the inhabitants of Neston parish.

The seven page document held in Cheshire Archives, records the reason for the petition:

It transpired that William Young and Theodore Cottingham 'churchwardens of Neston parish church' instigated the petition.
'On the grounds that Henry Wolstenholme and Samuel Ansdale also inhabitants of Neston and employed by them had begun to build a loft or gallery across the middle of the west end of the church prior to the plans being approved'

The build was to allow more light into the church and provide more pews or seats within, and a convenient staircase to access the area.

The allegation argued that it was dangerous and also costly to the inhabitants of Neston, and that the church timbers would so decay if rain were to be drawn into the church.

It was later confirmed by the Notary Publics (Public Officer) that no party had disturbed Henry Wolstenholme or Samuel Ansdale in the execution of the said order, and therefore were found not guilty of any temerity or contempt on the premises.

Neston's parishioners felt so strongly over their church that they put pen to paper to prevent the building of the gallery from continuing!
The following names were signed on the document;

William Young
Theodore Cottingham
Daniel Barrow
Henry Orrell
Thomas Charnock
William Wilson
William Johnson
Jacob Wolstenholme
George Bedson
William Hayes
Thomas Bolland

Joseph Burkley
Andrew Potter
John Bristoe
Thomas Johnson
Jane Wolstenholme
John Johnson
Jane Wilkinson
Thomas Belling
Ralph Bellin
Ester Bellin
Ann Rushton
Thomas Johnson
Martin Charnock
John Lightfoot
John Robinson
Thomas Wolstenholme
William Phillips
William Pickand
William Denson
Samuel Waring
Thomas Bristoe
Mary Green
Richard Waring
Blanch Curry
William Penkitt
Robert Jones
William Gordrey [Godfrey]
Samuel Charnock
William Norman
John Potter
Jane Penkitt
William Green
Thomas Hancock
Thomas Wittle
Elizabeth Edmondson
George Ridgate
Richard Gamon
Elizabeth Carter (witness)
George Calvelley (witness)
[Gal] Moulding (Notary Public)
Johannus Carter (Notary Public)
These names are in the same order as recorded on the document.

Interestingly Henry Wolstenholme was himself a church warden in 1723 and Samuel Ansdale in 1737!
Henry Wolstenholme was a grocer, he died in 1733; Samuel Ansdale lived in 'Park' Parkgate.

This gem of a document recording a local event concerning Neston's parish church, prior to the building of the present church.
In 1871 an inspection of the church showed that it was unsafe, and the main body of the church was taken down and rebuilt. Was this partly due to work that had begun on the gallery in 1726 I wonder?

Appendix 5

Vessel's in the Port of Chester 1740 – 1769

Reference QDN 1/5 Cheshire Archives and Local Studies (Cheshire Shared Services)

Between the years 1740 and 1769 the following vessels entered the Port of Chester situated along the River Dee.

1740 *Elizabeth John Jons*, 12 tons carrying cheese bound for Highlake (Hoylake).

1740 2 further ships at Parkgate both 35 tons, each carrying cheese.

1740 2 ships at Parkgate both 70 tons, each carrying cheese.

1741 4 ships at Parkgate:
100 ton ship *John Lyttler*, carrying cheese.
100 ton ship *Edward and Mary* carrying cheese.
Finch carrying 5½ tons of leather bound for Dublin.
Diligence, carrying cheese and potatoes.

1741 2 ships at Dawpool:
William and Sarah carrying 30 tons of cheese, the owner was William Glegg.
Levant Galley a 200 ton ship carrying 107 tons of leather, the owner was William Hooglands.

1742 *Lady Dorathea* a 200 tons ship carrying 44 tons of leather, its owner was Charles Delew.

1745 A Lighter to Dawpool carrying 3 tons of cheese, a second Lighter to Dawpool carrying cheese and leather.

1752 Dawpool 1Sloop for transporting cheese bound for London and Conway.
3 further Sloops carrying Cheese.

1753 Dawpool 8 Sloops were recorded.
1 was from Whitehaven carrying 15 ton of Corn for Bidston Mill!

1754 Dawpool 5 Sloops, no mention of cargoes.
Parkgate 4 Sloops, carrying cheese.

1755 Parkgate 7 Sloops were recorded, no cargoes mentioned

1756 Parkgate 3 Sloops were recorded, no cargoes mentioned
Dawpool 24 tons of grocery.
Dawpool 30 tons of leather.

1757 Parkgate only 1 ship carrying '*Mat*'!

1759 Parkgate 2 ships carrying skins and hide.

1760 Parkgate 2 ships carrying rigging and wine.

1762 Parkgate 5 ships carrying 40 tons of wine.
Skins
Tallow
Wine on a Lighter.
Skins on a Lighter.

1763 Dawpool 6 ships carrying:
10 tons of wine
10 tons of wine
24 tons of wine
27 tons of wine
10 tons of wine
5 tons of wine
Parkgate 1 ship carrying 30 tons of timber.

1764 Dawpool 5 Sloops with 200 bundles of leather to board the *Good Intent* bound for Lisbon.
Dawpool 5 Sloops with 200 bundles of leather to be put on *Nancy John* bound for Lisbon.
Dawpool 3 Sloops with 130 bundles of leather

1765 Parkgate 10 tons of wheat bound for Liverpool.

1766 Dawpool 27 tons of wine.
6 tons of leather.
Parkgate 10 tons of Manchester goods!

1768 Parkgate 9 tons of skins.
9 tons of bone.
15 tons of linen.

1769	Dawpool	21 tons of wine.
		10 tons of logwood.
	Parkgate	6 tons of tallow.
		20 tons of iron.

Iron was the last entry in the Port of Chester Vessel register for 1769; it's interesting to note the changes in the size of the ships able to anchor at the Ports on the River Dee. Also the change in cargo which was carried, particularly the last entry, iron, was this used for the new coal pit in Ness!

Appendix 6

Anglo - Saxon Churches in England

Many of the Anglo-Saxon churches were built of stone some were built of wood, listed below are some worthy of mentioning. If the churches were not destroyed by the Vikings or the Normans then some fell into disuse because the villages they were part of became uninhabited for one reason or another.

Greensted in Essex is the oldest wooden church in the country, the Oak palisade walls are sometimes classified as remnants of a palisade church or an early Stave church dating from the mid-9th or mid-11th century.

Brixworth in Northamptonshire the Church Of All Saints.
The building of the church is unclear although it was thought that the church came under attack by the Vikings in 870 AD. The church has been in constant use as a place of worship, due to its quiet location is one of the reasons it has been virtually unaltered over the centuries.

Bradford on Avon the Church of St Lawrence, the Saxon church is early 11th century and for many centuries the Saxon church was 'lost.' In 1715 it was used as an 'Ossuary' a place to house skulls and bones!.
In the 1800s it was used as a free school for boys, then in 1856 repair work uncovered two stone carved angels.
The stones are now known to be part of the original chancel arch; the church is still used today as a place of worship.

Escomb Church, the church was founded in 670-675 AD most of the stone came from the nearby Roman Fort of Binchester. One of the Roman stones is marked LEG VI 9sixth Legion).
It's actually set upside down, many of the stones exhibit Roman tool marks.
The church was restored in 1875-1880 and is now a Grade 1 listed building; a circular graveyard is another feature of an early Anglo-Saxon church.

Deerhurst Church in Gloucestershire was originally built in the late 7th century and has been altered many times, there are still some very interesting Anglo-Saxon features; the carved font is sculptured, there is an Anglo-Saxon Nave, a 9th century Apse, and a 10th century carving of an angel on the ruined tower.
There is plenty to keep one occupied here for quite a while.

St Peter–on-the-Wall Bradwell on Sea is another early Anglo-Celtic church the chapel originally was built in 654AD near the abandoned Roman Fort of OThona.

The church had been used as a barn there is evidence of this; the barn door has been cut into the walls! Then after the 1500s the church fell into disuse, it has now been restored and is a Grade 1 listed building. These are just of few of the early Anglo-Saxon churches you could visit; local churches with an ancient past are:

An example of some churches in Wirral

St Bridget's
The church in West Kirby, including the Dawson-Brown Museum, are well worth visiting, although the church you see on the outside is 19th century some parts inside are early 14th century. The museum holds a fine collection of ancient stones and artefacts. It is thought that a much earlier church stood on this site of Anglo-Saxon origin.

Chester Cathedral,
The ancient church was dedicated to Werburgh she was a 7th century saint and was born in Stone in Staffordshire. St Werburgh's remains were relocated to St Peter and St Paul within the city walls of Chester in 875, in 975 a monastery was built dedicated to St Werburgh and St Oswald.
In 1057 the church was rebuilt and became the protector and patron saint of the city.
There is a feast day on the 3rd February dedicated to St Werburgh.
It will take you the better part of the day to wander around the cathedral but it's well worth the effort.

Overchurch in Upton - there is no longer a church on the site; in 1709 the steeple was destroyed in a storm, two of the church bells were sold to provide funds for the repair of the church. In 1813 the church was pulled down, in the tree covered graveyard there are some four or five grave slabs buried in the undergrowth.

My mother took me to visit the graveyard over 45 years ago; we went armed with a toothbrush and a bottle of water. Kneeling down brushing away the moss and leaves from the large sandstone grave stones, thus revealing the epitaph of a boy drowned at sea, who had lived at 'Crabhall'.

This small act fuelled my deep interest in archaeology and family history from that time on.

Overchurch 'Overchirche' means church on the hill, an Anglo-Saxon Runic Stone was found on the site the stone reads:
'The people raised a memorial pray for Aethelmund.'
This was indeed a memorial to a respected leader, asking for prayers from passers-by, there was an Aethelmund recorded as a witness in a Mercian document, he was killed in Wessex in 800AD.

Did Aethelmund wander the tracks of Wirral? Did he beach his boat at Meols? Did he leave any descendants here?

As yet no other information shows any light on Aethelmund in Wirral, perhaps one day there may be!

Arial view of Hilbre Point and Red Rocks
Acknowledgment/credit to English Heritage (NMR) RAF Photography.

COTSWOLD
outdoor
Cotswold Outdoor
For all your outdoor clothing
and equipment needs
LIVERPOOL
CHESTER
Cotswold Outdoor Liverpool
58-60 Church Street, Liverpool, Merseyside L1 3AY
Tel. 01517 070323
Cotswold Outdoor Chester
82-84 Foregate Street, Chester, Cheshire CH1 1HB
Tel. 01244 400204
66 stores nationwide
0844 557 7755
cotswoldoutdoor.com
HH
MERRELL
Jack Wolfskin
bridgedale
Lowe alpine
THE NORTH FACE
MOUNTAIN HARD WEAR